What Your Mother Never Told You

A Survival Guide for Teenage Girls

ISBN: 1-4196-7869-8

ISBN-13: 9781419678691

Visit www.booksurge.com to order additional copies.

What Your Mother Never Told You

A Survival Guide for Teenage Girls

Richard M. Dudum

Island Publishing

Contents ~

Prologue   v

Letter to Teenage Girls   viii

Letter to Parents, Caregivers, and Counselors   x

PERCEPTIONS AND COMMUNICATION SKILLS   1

1. How Will You Be Remembered After High School?   3

2. Words and Actions   5

3. Body Language   7

4. Trust, Honesty, and Lies   9

5. Never Assume   13

6. Listen Closely and Don't Be Impressed By a Title   17

7. Beware of Opinions   19

WHO YOU ARE AND WHAT MAKES YOU TICK   21

8. What Kind of Soil Are You?   23

9. Figure Out Who You Are...NOT   25

10 Mean Girls   29

11. It's Not Just Peer Pressure   33

12. Change Friends When It's Time   35

13. Confidence and Self-Esteem   39

14. Change Your Attitude...Change Your Life   43

15. Why Do I Feel So Bad? 47

16. What Do Boys Really Think About Who You Are? 51

17. Don't Dress or Act Like a Ho 57

18. Respect Yourself 61

YOUR PARENTS 63

19. You Didn't Enter This World with a How-To Manual 65

20. I Don't Like My Parents' Behavior 67

21. Stereotypes 69

22. Just Do Your Best 71

23. Pick Your Fights 73

24. How to Tell Your Parents 75

HOW TO HANDLE YOURSELF 81

25. Trust Your Stomach 83

26. The Most Important Word in the Dictionary is "NO" 85

27. Always Have a Game Plan 87

28. Get Up and Leave 93

29. Let's Teach You How to Drink 97

30. Watch Your Back 101

31. Unwanted Attention 103

32. Gossip 107

33. Disrespectful Boys/Girls and Boyfriends 109

34. Easy or Hard 111

SEX, ALCOHOL, AND DRUGS 113

35. Sex, Alcohol, and Drugs—Do You Need Them? 115

36. Statistics 117

37. Drugs, Alcohol, and Your Body   121

38. Sexual Assault, Sexual Harassment, Rape   125

39. The Gray Area   129

40. Learn the Lesson, Grieve, Forgive Yourself,

    and Move Forward   133

THE MEDIA HYPE   **137**

41. Facebook, Email, Webcams   139

42. Sex and Porn in the Media and Internet   143

MANIPULATIVE BOYS   **147**

43. "You're Special"—That's Bullshit!   149

44. You Don't Owe Him Jack   153

RELATIONSHIPS AND SEX   **155**

45. What Will You Get by Giving a Blow Job or

    Having Anal Sex?   157

46. Why Are You Rushing to Have Sex?   163

47. Think Before the Morning After   169

48. Sex Is Often the Beginning of the End   171

CONSEQUENCES   **177**

49. Free Will   179

50. Alcohol is No Excuse for Bad Decisions   181

51. You Dodged a Bullet—This Time   185

52. Girls Have All the Power Over Boys   189

53. Wrong Place, Wrong Time   193

54. After Midnight   199

55. Don't Just Stand By and Watch—Do Something   201

56. How to Help a Friend in Need   205

HANG IN THERE AND GO FOR IT   **207**

57. Opportunities   209

58. The Graduating Boyfriend   211

59. Love   215

60. Adjust   219

61. This Book Is a Downer and Is Killing My Social Life   221

62. You Have a Blank Page   223

63. Allow Yourself to Be a Teenager   225

CLOSING THOUGHTS   **227**

Appendix A: Specific Drug Details   229

Appendix B: Sexual Assault—Steps to Take   231

Appendix C: Signs to Watch For   233

Appendix D: A Friend in Need   237

Appendix E: Take Some Time   241

Endnotes   243

Prologue ~

*L*et me introduce myself. I am a trial attorney, a realtor, a musician, a summer camp director, and a cancer survivor. I am a husband and the father of two sons and two daughters.

The best part of my life has been the past twenty-eight years working with teenagers and young adults, including my children. I've tried to provide them with tools I believe will help them successfully communicate and navigate through the turbulent teenage years. I've seen the success and failure of my efforts, both of which keep me going.

This book contains the thoughts and opinions I have discussed with hundreds of boys and girls, including my own children. My older daughter is in college and my younger daughter and her friends are starting high school. I've seen the same issues hurt so many girls so many times over the years that I decided to help by writing my insights, thoughts, and advice.

I want you to know from the onset that I speak very candidly, and at times, I am rather blunt. I apologize for some of my word choices. But you must understand that by reading, as opposed to listening, you are unable to hear the passion in my voice and feel the importance of my message. The passion for the protection of our children is reflected in my being frank and to the point.

My goal is to help girls anticipate issues and to provide strategies to address those issues; I use straightforward language that is easily understood and remembered. I have not watered down the importance of my message by attempting to be politically correct. I do not address the big-picture issues of feminism, women's rights, or the need to change how our culture and society treat and view girls and women. Rather, my efforts are focused on helping the girls to grow, to be strong, and to successfully deal with the realities that confront them *today*. At times, I do this by asking the girls to consider their future as well as the long-term consequences of their current actions.

Over the years, I've taken the time to listen to teenagers and young adults, and I understand what they say. I've taught them communication skills and common sense strategies that are in this book. I've seen them benefit and grow from our frank discussions and their use of these skills and strategies. I am not an expert on psychology or child development, but I am effective.

Teenage girls are very smart. They will get the point and understand what I am saying. They will make their most difficult decisions when their parents are not present. I believe this book will help them make the right choices in their lives, but the book alone is not enough.

I was so happy before I sent this book off for printing because I now had all my thoughts and advice in one book.

I told my younger daughter that if she needed help, all she had to do was read the book—"Check out Chapter 9; it's all there." Two days later, she said, "Dad, just because you wrote the book doesn't mean you should stop talking to me." I hugged her. She was right. I will never stop talking to her. I'm grateful she still needs and wants my help.

Finally, I have had the honor and privilege to help many teenagers and young adults over the years. I truly appreciate and thank all of you who previewed this book. I am grateful and proud of each and every one of you. As well, I am grateful to the middle school and high school counselors, the mother of four daughters who is the dean at an all-girls high school, as well as the internal medicine and pediatric physicians who provided their invaluable insights. Lastly, I thank my family for their love, thoughts, and patience.

Let's get started.

Dear Teenage Girl: (TAG)

This book is dedicated to YOU. I write it as if I've known you your whole life. Being a teenage girl and a young adult is not easy, but I promise that if you read this book and apply my strategies, your life will be a whole lot better.

I want you to know from the very beginning that there is a lot of tough love in this book. I say it like I see it, and I can be brutally honest. Your parents may not know that some of the things I write about are actually happening. They may believe that some chapters don't apply to you, and they *may be* right. But *you* will know better—that's why I wrote the book for you. It contains information that you *absolutely* need to know, *even though you might rather not,* and even though not all of it applies to you!

I know that, at times, this book will make you tired and even upset. When that happens, take a break, regroup, and then come back for more. You've got what it takes to handle anything that life throws at you, including the tough love in my message.

I am writing this book for you because I want you to be yourself and to live life on your own terms. I want you to understand and always respect yourself. I want you to realize the power and control you have over what happens in your life. I want you to be cautious and to protect yourself. I want you to set and meet your own expectations. You have gifts and talents that you have yet to discover.

At the same time, you are at serious risk; you are vulnerable and susceptible to manipulation. You are uncertain about who you are, where you fit in, and what's expected of you. There are those who can easily take advantage of you or manipulate you. I don't want that to happen. I want to help you help yourself. I want to help you be yourself. You are not lost—you're just finding your way.

It is my belief that good communication skills are the key to your success and survival. The chapters in this book revolve around how you communicate through your words, actions, and body language, and how you, in turn, are perceived. I focus on the choices you face and the known, and often unknown, consequences of your decisions.

This book addresses issues that you are, or will soon be, facing. These issues, like the chapters in this book, often overlap. The first time you confront these issues is often the most difficult. My goal is to empower you by alerting you to these concerns and providing you with strategies that will enable you to successfully navigate your teenage and young adult years.

Be patient. The book starts slowly as we review the essential communication skills that will help you with the later chapters. Hang in there with me; starting with Chapter 9, you will quickly get to each and every issue on your mind. As for you older teens, please don't stop reading. Yes, you may have already been exposed to many of these issues, but the book includes information that will help you *well into your twenties.*

I want you to know that what I have written in this book has been on my mind for a very long time, but no matter what I write, *YOU are still the one making all the decisions.* The only difference is that after reading this book, you will know and understand the rules of the game. How you apply those rules and live your life is entirely up to you. *The ball is in your court!*

I recommend that you reread *What Your Mother Never Told You* at the beginning of each of your high school and college years just to remind yourself of the rules and strategies. *With every year that you mature, this book will grow with you and actually take on a different and deeper meaning.* You will better understand yourself and the message I am trying to communicate. *That's why it's so important to read the entire book for a second and third time.* I hope and pray that it touches you in a positive way. If you like what you read, and if it helps you in any way, please touch someone else by passing it along.

TAG, you're it!

Dear Parents, Caregivers, and Counselors:

If you are reading this book, in my opinion, you are well on your way to becoming a more successful parent and/or mentor.

We are a generation of helicopter parents who hover over and excessively tend to our children. This can backfire. We are not doing them a favor when we hide them from the issues of today. We cannot pretend that the issues discussed in this book are not happening. We can't turn away and act as if we don't hear or see what's going on in our schools and homes.

Our daughters are especially vulnerable when they are introduced to the real world without being adequately prepared. They are curious, playful, intelligent, and beautiful. They look and often act much older than their age. They are getting the wrong kind of attention much earlier than they should. They will find themselves in difficult situations that will test them over and over again. Have you adequately prepared them?

Sometimes we are not comfortable discussing delicate issues with our daughters. Whose job is it, Mom's or Dad's?

Often the most delicate issues are left unaddressed, and we live with the blind hope that somehow, somewhere, they will learn how to take care of themselves.

The problem is that when we don't take the time to raise and discuss delicate issues, our daughters will learn the hard way. They will learn from the wrong people. They will have the wrong experiences. Worst of all, they will rarely tell us when the problem arises. They don't know how to approach us. How can we expect them to talk to us when we never take the time to fully talk with them?

Much of this is not our fault. We are all working hard to provide for and care for our children. Time constraints are often overwhelming. We are often unwilling to admit what's happening to our children at such a young age. How can we expect to help them help themselves if we are unaware or in denial? Maybe we don't know how to help them. We need to do more than just hope things will work out.

Our children need our time, our presence, our love, and our attention. Logically, we often give the most attention to the child who needs the most help. Often these are our kids who seem to have the most difficult time. Don't ignore the needs of your other children. *I find that the child who seems to be the most capable and appears to be doing well is often the one most in need of our love and attention.* Keep a watchful eye. Don't let anyone get lost in the shuffle.

Your daughters are like flowers. Tend to them and they will grow strong and beautiful. Listen to them. Talk *to* them, not *at* them. Make a point to let them know how proud you are when they do good things, work hard, and make good choices. *Constantly teach and remind them to respect themselves.* Acknowledge and encourage them often. Show and tell them you love them. Let them know you're there for them and make a point to actually be there.

Don't be a bystander; instead, go through adolescence with your child. Do your best to schedule your family first and everything else second. Create opportunities to spend quality time with them—movies, shopping, lunch, even playing cards. Watch *their* TV shows with them and drive to and from their events—what you watch and hear will give you insights into their world. Also, try *not* to leave them unattended too often and for too long—that's when things go wrong.

Create an environment where your daughter feels comfortable telling you *everything*. Don't be impulsive and overreact when you hear what she says—especially if what you hear disappoints and upsets you. Remember, it was hard for her to confide in you in the first place. If your daughter does confide in you and there is little if anything you can do to help her correct a mistake she has made, then hug her, tell her you love her, and try not to get angry with her. Discuss the mistake, why it happened and how to avoid it in the future. Keep this in mind when you read Chapter 24, *How to Tell Your Parents*. At the same time, make a point to remember *who you were and what you did when you were her same age*—tough love is *not* an option here.

It is our responsibility to teach our children everything within our ability. We have to prepare them to move forward in life without us. We have to teach them to advocate for themselves. They need to know what to expect and how we expect them to respond when trouble comes their way. They need to learn how to anticipate problems. *We have only a short period of time to teach them all they need to know*. This book is a good first step.

If I had my way, some of the topics discussed in this book would have been better left unsaid; however, because our children are in the midst of these issues and in the eye of this storm, I do *not* have that luxury. You may not like some of the topics I discuss. You may not be interested in my opinions. I am certain there are times you will disagree with my approach and choice of language. That's OK. I didn't write the book for you; this book is for our *daughters.* Use it as a starting point to raise and discuss issues at home. You can also refer to it if and when any of these issues come up. More likely, they will never be raised and that's the main reason I wrote this book.

I recommend that you leave a copy next to your daughter's bed a few weeks before the start of high school, or even earlier if you deem necessary. Many of the girls previewing this book actually told me that they were exposed in middle school to the issues I discuss. If you decide to hold off, the winter break of high school freshman year is the absolute latest to get this information in her hands.

Your daughters will no longer be dealing with childhood issues when they enter high school. Their sophomore year in high school and freshman year in college could be even worse; that's when they know just enough to be careless and dangerous in their high school or college environments.

Remember, our daughters need to know how to take care of themselves when we are not there. To help her along the way, get to know her friends, her friends' parents, and her whereabouts. Make sure that you and the parents of your daughter's friends are on the same page, especially in regard to parties and sleepovers. *And don't believe everything you hear!*

As for you moms, please don't be offended by the title of this book. A fifteen-year-old girl suggested the title, even though she has a wonderful relationship with her mother.

On a side note, I anticipate that some of you may be reading this book long before your daughters are in high school. I understand your effort to get a jump-start, but I don't know if you are ready to consider what I have to say. If you are a parent of a child not yet in high school, you may not appreciate the urgency and value of my message. If that's the case, please reread this book one month before the start of your child's high school freshman year, and leave her a copy.

Finally, I have not yet written a guide for *teenage* boys addressing their roles and responsibilities relating to the issues I raise. I've discussed this on numerous occasions with many of you, and I agree that a boy's book is long overdue. Until then, my advice is that you teach your sons to always respect themselves, respect their bodies, respect their families, friends, and other people. And *always* respect women. Teach them through your words and actions. You can use almost every chapter in this book as a guide to begin and to continue teaching those concepts to your sons.

~

Perceptions and Communication Skills

How Will You Be Remembered After High School?　　3

Words and Actions　　5

Body Language　　7

Trust, Honesty, and Lies　　9

Never Assume　　13

Listen Closely and Don't Be Impressed By a Title　　17

Beware of Opinions　　19

Chapter One ~

How Will You Be Remembered After High School?

Other than being a place of learning, high school is all about image—who you are, how you look, what you wear, who you know, and what you do. How you act and treat people during high school is how you will be remembered by your classmates and peers years later. It's true. If you were mean or promiscuous in high school or college, your peers will always remember you as being mean or promiscuous in five, ten, twenty, and even thirty years from now.

In the eyes of your peers, it doesn't matter that later in life you have grown, matured, and changed. The initial perception that your peers and classmates will have of you in years to come will be those EXACT characteristics that you communicated and demonstrated in school.

Why does this matter? Because you get only one chance to make a first impression. As you move through the stages of your life, it's a lot easier being remembered as a person of high caliber, genuine character, and having a reputation that accurately reflects who you are as opposed to having to overcome a negative perception that you created when you were too young to know better. Unfortunately, the bad things you do will often be remembered most, but you can avoid and change that *if you choose to.*

You have complete control over your destiny *right now.* If you want, you have the power to turn things around and make positive changes in your life and in the lives of people around you. Your future is not carved in stone at this moment in time. You have the ability to choose the path you take and the opportunity to make quality changes along the way. It's totally within your grasp to make good things happen every day of your life, starting with today—*today is the first day of the rest of your life.*

High school and college are times to remember, not times to forget and regret. Wherever you go, whatever you do, try to make yourself a better person, and in turn, your world will be a better place. What you put out in life will come back. People will remember you.

Chapter Two ～

Words and Actions

Your teenage years are a time to grow, to learn about yourself and other people, and to learn how to have good relationships with your parents, teachers, and friends.

It's also a time to learn about people and relationships that you want absolutely nothing to do with. It's a time when you learn how to take the steps necessary to protect yourself and to avoid communication, interaction, and situations with those people you *don't* want to be a part of your life.

The key to having good relationships is good communication. You communicate through your words and actions.

Your words are very important. People will hear them and listen to you. Your words are the window to your true character. Your words reflect what you think and how you feel. They allow the listener to understand you and evaluate your trust, honesty, integrity, and sincerity. Choose your words carefully. They will be remembered.

Your actions actually speak louder than your words. Your actions also reflect what you think and feel, and reveal your trustworthiness and honesty. If you don't do what you say, your words have little or no value; they are empty and meaningless. You can have a beautiful smile and a lovely personality, but those qualities will carry you only so far and for so long. *If you don't mean it, don't say it.* If you say you're going to do something, do it. A contradiction between your words and actions calls into question your credibility.

People know who you are by what you say and what you do. I want you to *fully* understand that your words and actions not only touch the people around you but also impact and change their lives.

In all of your relationships, always say what you mean, always mean what you say, and always do what you say.

Chapter Three ～

Body Language

Communication can be both verbal and nonverbal. Be aware of how loudly you speak without ever saying a word.

"Body language" is communication by nonverbal behavior, gestures, and body movements. Although you may be silent, your body can be speaking loudly and clearly by sending out signals. At the same time, the people you communicate with are also sending out verbal as well as nonverbal signals and cues.

Effective communication requires that you be able to read between the lines of people's words in order to better understand their inner thoughts. Equally important is becoming aware of and understanding what nonverbal messages you are sending and how they are being interpreted.

Examples of body language and how it can be interpreted include rolling your eyes (disapproval), crossing your arms (anger), slouching in a chair (tired/bored), tapping your fingers (impatience), biting your nails (nervous), tilting your head (interest), resting your head in your hand (boredom), holding your hand to your cheek (thinking), standing tall (confidence), looking away (boredom, disapproval), touching your hair (lack of self-confidence, insecurity, boredom), glancing around (curiosity, assessment, shyness, interest), and twirling/tossing your hair and crossing your legs (flirting). The list goes on and on.

Be aware that body language can send mixed signals. If someone is crossing their arms, is that person upset or just cold? Don't jump to conclusions. You have to interpret both a person's words and as many nonverbal "signals" as possible before you decide what is being communicated.

Your body language can get you into all sorts of trouble. Take a minute and think about what you do when you send a negative nonverbal message. You made your point without ever saying a word! That can lead to problems if you don't realize the nonverbal messages you are communicating.

Do your best to become aware of when and how your body is sending messages. Then try to control your nonverbal communication to avoid sending the wrong messages and to better reflect who you are, what you are trying to communicate, and how you want to be perceived.

Chapter Four ～

Trust, Honesty, and Lies

*L*et's talk a minute about trust, honesty, and lies.

You know that your words and actions have meaning in your relationships. Your parents, teachers, and friends rely on you to be genuine and honest. You build trust and loyalty in your relationships when you're honest. Lies undermine that trust. Lies hurt, disappoint, and can demonstrate your betrayal and disrespect. They often cause the victim of your lies to lose respect for, and trust in, you.

Lies can come in the form of words, actions, or silence. Everyone knows what it means to lie using words. These are active lies, where you consciously make the decision to not, and actually don't, tell the truth.

Lying through actions is less active but still a problem. Lying through actions can occur when you say one thing and do another. I understand that sometimes things don't work out, and that what you say and what you do may be different. Just keep in mind that it's very important to make every effort to do what you say. You lose credibility when you don't.

There is another form of lying. If you fail to say something or tell someone the truth while knowing that you should speak up and tell the truth, you are lying by your silence. Unlike words and actions, which allow someone to see and hear obvious signs of lying, silence is passive lying.

Please keep in mind that lying in any form can damage your relationships. The greater the lie, the greater the harm, and the more serious the consequence. Lies are based on your intentions. When you actively mislead or passively withhold, you are lying. If you decide to or have to tell the truth, then tell the whole truth. A half-truth is another lie.

I understand that no one is perfect. We all make mistakes and tell an occasional lie. Sometimes we can be so upset by something that we believe we have no choice but to lie. It could be something we want to forget—we don't know what else to do. But there *is* something you can do. You can tell the truth and prevent further damage to your relationships. You can stop yourself before you get into the habit of lying. You can prevent lies from compounding and prevent situations from becoming even worse.

I want you to make every effort to build trust and honesty and avoid lies in all of your relationships. If you have made a mistake and have lied about it, and *if* the mistake and lie are absolutely NOT the person you truly are, then *I want you to tell the person you lied to that you are **not** a liar*—you made a mistake. But please, say this *only* if it's absolutely true. Otherwise it's—*just*—*another*—*lie*. After admitting your mistake, make a point to **demonstrate and define who you truly are through your future words and actions**.

Lies hold you hostage. Truth sets you free. Truth is the most basic requirement of trust and honesty. Trust and honesty are the foundation of all solid relationships. If there is a crack in that foundation, sooner or later that house will come tumbling down. Trust is fragile. Once broken, trust is not easy, sometimes impossible, to repair. If lost, it takes time, effort, sincerity, honesty, credibility, integrity, respect for the other person, and self-respect to rebuild trust.

To some, lying is an acceptable way to live. To others, it's not an option. Only you decide which person you want to be.

Chapter Five ～

Never Assume

Never assume that you know what someone is thinking or feeling. Never! Never assume that the other person knows what you are thinking and feeling. When you "assume" you make an "ass" out of "u" and "me."

In all your relationships, make every effort to listen closely to hear and understand what someone is saying to you. Don't be so presumptuous as to think that you *already* know what's on their mind. You're probably missing much more than you realize, and you may be totally wrong!

In addition to listening, use your words to communicate; you absolutely won't be understood unless you explain your thoughts and feelings. Communicate simply and clearly to make sure your thoughts, feelings, and intentions are clear. If it's important, never leave it unsaid.

If you are unsure of what to say or how to say it, write down your thoughts. By writing, you will better understand how you feel about something and what you want to communicate. Use simple words. Ask yourself while you are writing,

Do I fully understand what I'm trying to communicate? Will the person I am trying to communicate with fully understand what I am trying to say? If not, rewrite it.

Don't wait too long to say what you have to say or write. Delay only makes matters worse. Make the first move. You may not get a second chance to say what's on your mind. When you stop talking and stop communicating, your relationship could begin to unravel, and the opportunity to better the situation may be lost.

Imagine this: Your boyfriend is very upset or quiet. When you ask what's wrong, you don't get an answer, or you get an incomplete answer. You keep asking but get nowhere. You struggle to figure out and fully understand what he's thinking and why he is acting this way. You get frustrated, upset, and even angry because you want to help and understand what's wrong, but you are not being allowed to. You start wondering and assuming all kinds of things. You then get angry with him for things that you are assuming—things that may have nothing to do with his silence. To retaliate, you become silent. This has now evolved into a vicious cycle that presents a serious danger to the success of any relationship. Never assume. Avoid silence. Communicate.

Another scenario arises when both you and the other person know that something more needs to be said about an issue, but there is only silence or incomplete communication between you. Something remains unsaid. The longer the silence, the more assumptions come into play. The person needing to hear more makes an assumption interpreting your silence as meaning the subject is really not important to you, that you don't really care, and that this person is not worthy of further discussion or explanation from you. The person may be wrong, but he or she doesn't know it.

This may not seem like a problem now, but it is. You must always communicate. If the matter is not fully discussed, fully resolved, and made old history, it will always linger. Your relationship will be extremely fragile. It will be more at risk than you might realize, especially the next time there is tension in your relationship. If it's important, fix it now.

If you have something to say, say it, even if what you say risks hurting the other person. Don't hold back. The passage of time will not make it go away. Get it all out so you can put it to rest and behind you for your and the other person's benefit. It's only then that your relationship with that person will truly move forward.

Never assume. Avoid silence. Never stop listening. Never stop talking. Communicate.

Chapter Six ⁓

Listen Closely and Don't Be Impressed By a Title

*A*s you already know, everyone has two ears and one mouth. That means you should listen twice as much as you talk. Everyone knows how to talk. Few people know how to listen.

Listen to people you trust. I know that your first instinct is to talk to your friends when you have a problem. Be careful. Your friends probably don't know how to handle the situation any better than you. In fact, your friends may only complicate matters and mess things up. It's always better to speak directly to the person with whom you're having a problem, rather than through your friends. Sometimes talking with friends can cause more confusion and drama.

Another thing: If someone you trust says something that you don't think is right or acts in ways that you truly question, BEWARE. Don't ignore your concern and good sense. Something may be very, very wrong. Watch yourself and them closely. Protect yourself. Stay away from them if you're not comfortable. *Always avoid situations that could put you in harm's way.* Danger can present itself in many forms and through many people, even the people closest to you whom you *think* you can and *should* be able to trust.

I am not trying to be cynical or to make you paranoid. I am only trying to alert you to and protect you from sad realities in our world.

Just because someone is a father or a mother, a sister or a brother, an uncle or an aunt, a cousin, a longtime family friend or a friend's parent, a priest, a coach, a police officer, a doctor, or a teacher does not mean that you can automatically trust him or her.

Here are a few incidents that make my point:

"After years of legal wrangling, the nation's largest Roman Catholic archdiocese may finally move to settle hundreds of clergy sex abuse claims against it..." [1]

A man "who coached girls' youth soccer and softball admitted yesterday that he molested seven of his players..." [2]

"...a veteran police officer used excessive force on citizens in four separate incidents in the past nine months." [3]

"A former high school band teacher was sentenced to a year in County Jail after pleading no contest to having sex with a 17-year-old female student." [4]

A title alone does not make a person trustworthy.

Always take the time to listen, but listen closely enough to decide whether what you hear makes good sense. You have the ability to evaluate people and situations if you take the time to watch and listen closely.

Chapter Seven ~

Beware of Opinions

I absolutely want you to beware of opinions.

Have you ever heard someone try to add credibility to their point of view by saying, "*They* say ..."? Every time I hear that phrase, I ask myself, *Who's they?* I've never been very impressed by "they." What do "they" know that I don't? Please keep in mind that the person giving his or her opinion may have little, if anything, of value to contribute.

Here is the rule: *Always take a close look at exactly WHO is giving the opinions.* Is it someone you can trust? Does the person actually know better? Is he or she making any sense? Think twice before deciding whose opinion should be considered. Don't trust blindly. Not everyone knows what he or she is talking about. Determine for yourself how much weight and value you give to people and their opinions.

If the opinions are of little or no value, disregard them and don't include them in your decision-making process. If you don't hold the people giving the opinions in high regard, dismiss their opinions entirely.

Get opinions ONLY from people you trust. Get opinions from people who actually do know better than you. And if they do know better, then listen to and consider the value of that opinion when making your decisions.

Who You Are and
What Makes You Tick

What Kind of Soil Are You?   23

Figure Out Who You Are...NOT   25

Mean Girls   29

It's Not Just Peer Pressure   33

Change Friends When It's Time   35

Confidence and Self-Esteem   39

Change Your Attitude...Change Your Life   43

Why Do I Feel So Bad?   47

What Do Boys Really Think About Who You Are?   51

Don't Dress or Act Like a Ho   57

Respect Yourself   61

Chapter Eight ~

What Kind of Soil Are You?

*T*his is *not* a book about religion, but I believe the following short parable is very relevant to your personal growth.

Jesus told a story comparing SEED to the GOSPEL, and SOIL to those who HEAR the gospel. In simple terms, He told this story to teach us that the key to spiritual growth is the *willingness* of the person receiving or hearing the gospel to listen, learn, and grow.

I believe that *the key to your personal growth is your willingness to listen to, and consider* the importance of, the information I am trying to communicate. If you are hard soil or rock, then you won't listen and the seeds I throw will *not* grow. You will learn little, if anything. If you are sandy soil, you may get some limited benefit from this book, but not enough. If you choose to be good fertile soil, you will benefit most and grow from the seeds that are being thrown. You will listen, understand, and do your best to **be who you are, and who you want to be.**

As you read the following chapters ask yourself, *What kind of soil am I?*

Are you willing to receive the message that I am trying to communicate? It's totally up to you. It's your life.

Chapter Nine ~

Figure Out Who You Are... NOT

All teenagers want to figure out who they are. That's part of growing up, but it's no easy task. If you don't yet know who you are, it's much easier to figure out *who you're NOT*. It's so simple. You can better understand what you do and don't believe by figuring out who you are NOT and what you DON'T want to do.

Every time you face a difficult decision ask yourself, *Is this the person I want to be?* If not, then you just figured out who you are NOT as it relates to that one issue. You are now one step closer to figuring out who you are.

Let's consider some of the issues that surround you right now. Are you the girl who looks down on, or thinks you're better than, other girls who look different from you? Are you the person who lies, cheats, or steals? Are you the person who gets drunk or gets high? Are you the girl who wants to dress up for and be the show at your friends' lingerie party or to engage in sex? Are you the person who wants to lie to your parents? Are you the girl who's an angel at home and promiscuous when you leave the house?

It makes total sense that you're different with your friends. But if there's a drastic difference between your behavior at home and away from home, you must take the time to understand what you're doing and why. Will your parents understand the difference? Do YOU understand the difference? Which person are you or do you want to be?

Are you the insecure girl who needs a boyfriend to validate your self-worth or to rationalize having sex? Maybe you haven't figured out that right now *you don't need a boyfriend* at all! You will meet more people and have a far better time just being yourself, without a boyfriend.

Will you swap boys with your friends or make-out or hook-up with any guy who smiles at you, even if you don't really know him or don't want to be in a real relationship with him? I define "hook-up" to mean almost everything short of sex. Maybe your friends want to make-out for no reason. Is that you? Take a minute and really think about it. What's the purpose? Does it have any meaning? Is it fulfilling? Or does it just kill your reputation?

Many teenagers will do one or more of these things. Do you or your friends? If not, you're ahead of the game and on the right track. If you do, take a minute and ask yourself, *Is this who I want to be?*

As you figure out who you are, **always do what's right for you based on *your* values, *your* expectations, *your* goals, and *your* priorities**. Every time you do the right thing, the right thing becomes easier to do. Look deep inside yourself for guidance and answers. Your answers are all right there waiting for you.

Consider this idea: Keep a journal called "Who I Am *Not*, Who I Am and Want to Be." Draw a line down the middle of a blank piece of paper making two columns. On the top left side, write "Who I Am Not." On the top right side, write "Who I Am and Want to Be." In the left column, list all the things you don't want as part of your life. Add to that list what you learned on that day about who you are *NOT and who you don't want to be.* In doing so, you are defining who you actually are; write that in the opposite right column. You won't have to do this for very long; each entry will help you better understand who you are not, and in turn, who you actually are.

By the way, you don't have to wait for something bad to happen to make a good entry in the right column. Make a point to add ALL of your accomplishments, ALL of the good things you do, and EVERYTHING you are grateful for and that makes you feel proud about yourself in the right-hand column. Then watch that column grow!

Don't stress about finding yourself; you're not lost. You are simply figuring out who you are, one issue at a time. **You figure out who you are by your actions and decisions.**

I know it's not easy figuring out who you are with all of these issues around you, but everything will be OK. You have so much depth inside of you. Look deep into your heart. You already know what's right and wrong. All you have to do is believe in, and be, yourself. As you better understand who you are *not,* it will become easier for you to focus your positive thoughts on the beautiful young lady that you already are.

Chapter Ten ～

Mean Girls

I don't know why, but some girls are mean. They say and do hurtful things to you and to each other. They give looks and attitude as sharp as a knife. They look down at you and walk right by you as if you don't exist. They even make nasty or degrading comments about you, your friends, or the people you love.

It hurts when they act this way. It hurts when you're excluded, made to feel invisible, and isolated. It's no fun when you're not part of "the group." It doesn't make sense when girls who are supposed to be your friends suddenly change and turn on you.

Why do some girls act this way? Maybe they think they have more than you, and you're not worthy of their attention. Maybe they don't like something you said or did. Maybe they are jealous and want something you have: your boyfriend, your looks, your talent, your reputation, your family, your brains, or your grades. Maybe they are just shallow or spoiled brats! Who really knows why they are so mean?

It would be nice to understand what motivates them. Maybe there is no answer. Maybe they're just being bitches.

It's not so simple to deal with girls like this. You just want to fit in. You're often self-conscious and confused. You're not quite sure what you have to do and how you have to act to fit in. Sometimes it seems that we all want to be someone else. What do you do?

Let's think about this for a minute. Do these girls even know you? Have they taken the time to talk to you? Have they made any effort to understand who you are and what makes you tick? The answers are probably *no*. And if they're *yes*, they probably *still* don't know you!

Are you willing to change your behavior or who you are to become part of their group? Are you willing to sacrifice your true self to be more like them? ABSOLUTELY NOT. Don't change yourself for others. Don't lower yourself to their level. You are who you are, and if they don't like it, that's not your problem.

It's perfectly normal that you question and doubt yourself. Everybody does. I want you to know that there is absolutely nothing wrong with you. Nothing is expected of you. You never have to compromise your values and your morals to be like them.

I want you to realize that you are not alone. All teenagers are unsure and insecure about themselves. Most girls in your school feel the same way you do. It may be hard to believe, but even the most popular, the coolest, and, yes, even those mean girls are insecure. Mean girls put you down in order to hold themselves up.

How do you handle mean girls? Here's the rule: *Try your best to simply not bother with girls who act this way toward you.* That's right—learn to let it go. If they want the spotlight, let them have it. Don't waste your time wondering why they act that way. That's not your problem; it's theirs. When they act that way, they are not worth your time.

Never change who you are and what you think to accommodate someone else. You're fine just being you. Soon you will realize that you are better off without them.

Try this strategy: If how they act is *not* directly affecting you, just ignore them, smile, hold your head up high, and walk on by. Let them look and talk. Let them make their mistakes. YOU be elegant. Just walk on by.

However, if how they act *is* having a direct impact on you, don't tolerate it. I'm not telling you to get into fights with other girls. I'm not telling you to touch or hurt anybody. Use your words and clearly communicate to them that what they are saying or doing is absolutely NOT OK with you. Be assertive, not aggressive. You don't need permission to say what's on your mind.

It's important for you to realize that when you are defending yourself verbally, and you speak with an intelligent, sensible, and well-thought-out response, you will probably be met by silence. The mean girls will realize their faults (even though they won't admit it). You will have set the tone and earned respect from the mean girls.

I understand that being assertive and speaking up does not work for everyone. If that's not your style, then do what works best for you. Walk away. Move on to better things. Do whatever you need to do. If these strategies don't work and you need help, talk to your teachers, school counselors and parents. Get the help you need. Don't let anyone mess with you.

By the way, don't confuse being pretty or popular with being mean. Many popular and pretty girls are friends with different people in different groups. They respect themselves and other girls. They don't go around hurting, excluding, or putting down other girls. Many popular girls are understanding and empathetic and can put themselves in other people's shoes. Don't prejudge someone just because she is pretty.

One last point: If you are dating a boy, and other girls are jealous, don't be surprised if mean girls tell you stories or start rumors about that boy or about you. They will make up all kinds of nonsense to upset you and interfere with your relationship. They are jealous that you have what they want. They are trying to trick you into saying or doing something careless. Tell the boy you're dating what you heard and take it from there. *Don't let the mean girls win by creating problems that actually don't exist.* That's what mean girls do. (By the way, manipulative boys are capable of doing the exact same thing if *they're* jealous and want to *get* with you.)

Let me ask you some questions: Are you a mean girl? Have you treated another girl unfairly? Think about how you hurt that person. Is that really who you want to be? If not, tell her you're sorry. If you owe someone an apology, apologize now. Really think about the reputation you have at this point in time. If it's not the reputation you want, you still have time right now to change how you act, how you treat people, how you are perceived, and how you will be remembered.

Remember, what you put out will come back.

Chapter Eleven —

It's Not Just Peer Pressure

Your parents want to protect you from peer pressure. You may laugh it off because you don't think you're susceptible to peer pressure. Let me help you understand what I mean when I say "misery loves company."

If your friends get drunk, high, randomly make-out, have sex, cut school, lie, steal, cheat, are rebellious for no reason, or engage in any other questionable activity, it's so much easier for them to feel better about themselves and their actions if they know they are not alone. Why? Even though they may not realize it, misery loves company.

Your friends may not be trying to hurt you. They simply don't want to be alone in the mistakes they make—misery loves company.

Your friends may encourage you to directly or indirectly make the same mistakes they have already made or are thinking about making. They may tell you how great it is or was, and may ask if you've been there yet. They may tell you what you're missing out on. They may imply that there is something wrong with you because you haven't done x, y, or z, or because you're not doing x, y, and z. They're wrong! Misery loves company.

Don't help your friends justify their bad decisions by you repeating their poor choices. We ALL will make our own mistakes in life, and yes, hopefully you will learn and grow from your mistakes. Think it through—don't add your friends' mistakes to your own.

Never let someone else think for you. Please, don't allow yourself to pay for someone else's mistakes! Don't let your friends or anyone else influence you in the wrong way. You have a brain. Use it. Only you decide what doors you want to open and when.

Make your *own* decisions.

Chapter Twelve ~

Change Friends When It's Time

A friend is someone you can trust and who will always be there for you. That friend will listen to you, respect you, and help you in times of need. A friend will disagree with you when she thinks you're wrong and will betray your secret and seek outside help for you when she truly fears for your safety and well-being. Your friend will dance with you, laugh with you, cry with you, hide with you, play with you, pray with you, party with you, and will always keep your safety and well-being in mind.

It's hard to find good friends. At some point in everyone's life, there comes a time when you need to shuffle and change friends. When that time comes, you have a decision to make. It may be time to make new friends and sometimes distance yourself from old friends who no longer share your interests. These old friends now become acquaintances.

It's hard to change friends, but sometimes that's what you need to do when who you are *now* is different from the people around you. This is especially true if your "friends" no longer have most of the above qualities and their only value is that they represent a social group that you are or were in, or still want to be a part of. In that circumstance, they are not truly your friends at all, and maybe it's time to make a change.

I know it's important to be accepted in high school and college. So many girls want to be popular or associate with a particular group. Your childhood friends may be part of that group. It's difficult to change friends when you have grown up with these girls, but they no longer reflect who you want to be. I want you to know that it's perfectly okay to change friends if you have grown and become a different person.

Think about it: Maybe you haven't changed at all—you've simply decided to be true to yourself, and/or you now have a different definition of "fun." Either way, never feel obligated to remain close friends. Although you may have history with a friend, that's in the past. Your future is unwritten. Your future is what you make it, and your story is affected by who's around you.

Challenge yourself to pick good friends and to change friends when the time is right. There are girls in your school who are just like you. Like you, they want quality friends who want to make good choices. Challenge yourself to change friends if you no longer agree with what they do. Make a point to distance yourself from someone when you know it's the right thing for you. Surround yourself with friends who reflect who you are and who you aspire to be—friends who bring out the very best in you and who don't bring you down and possibly damage your reputation simply by your being associated with them. You will be a lot happier being with people who allow you to be yourself.

One last point: If you find that your friends are distancing themselves from YOU, take a close look at YOUR behavior. Maybe you are saying or doing things differently, negatively. Maybe you are not being a good example or a good friend. Maybe they are realizing that you are no longer like them. This could be a good thing if these are people you want to distance yourself from, or a bad thing if you want to remain close friends with them.

Take a close look at where you've been, where you're at now, where you're going next, who's been there, and who will be there with you—are you in good company?

Seek out good friends and be a good friend. Change friends when it's time to do so. If you're fortunate enough to have only one true friend, then you are the luckiest person in the world.

Chapter Thirteen ~

Confidence and Self-Esteem

It's not easy having confidence and self-esteem when you're in transition. "Transition" means that you are evolving, changing, growing, and learning new concepts. To understand what's happening, *you must make an effort to be aware that you are in transition.* Transition takes time.

It may sound corny, but I sometimes think that a teenage girl is like a butterfly. The life cycle of a butterfly involves a remarkable series of changes. There's a huge transition from caterpillar to butterfly in a very short time. The same thing is happening to you. Everything is changing inside you as well as all around you in your teenage years.

You are trying to figure out who you are and where you fit in. You're learning and enjoying the new freedom that comes with getting older. At the same time, you are beginning to understand and appreciate life's details, responsibilities, and the consequences of everything you do. You're dealing with boys, mean girls, parents, school, peer pressure, friends, and relationships. You're curious and are trying to figure out how you feel about yourself, sex, alcohol, drugs, and other people.

You may feel rebellious. You get angry and don't like being told what to and what not to do. You're learning about who you want and *do not* want in your life. Your body is changing every day. Some days are good, and some are bad. You are becoming more aware of things in this world that you like and dislike. You are becoming an adult, and you are being prepared for even more responsibility. You're no longer swimming in the shallow water; the water is getting deeper and the waves are getting choppy.

Don't let transition scare you. It becomes a problem *only* if you rush yourself and try to grow up too fast. Try not to get overwhelmed by the uncertainty of who you are right now, where you're headed, or who you are becoming. *The best way to battle your insecurities is to notice what's happening to and around you, and understand how you feel about these things.* **Be more aware.** That's the key to confidence and self-esteem.

The more you understand yourself, your parents, your relationships and the world, the more trust you will have in yourself. As you trust yourself more, your faith in your abilities will grow. You will become more confident. You will feel better about yourself. You will develop self-esteem. You will make conscious, thoughtful decisions as opposed to making confused, pressured, and anxiety-driven choices. You won't act like a machine and just let things happen without thinking about what you're doing and why.

Remember that you are absolutely not the only one going through these changes. You're not in transition alone. Realize that everybody around you is doing the exact same thing. But they may *not* be aware of what's happening to them. They may be figuring themselves out in an entirely different way.

Notice the people who are more careless, more aggressive, and more extreme; that's *their* way of dealing with transition. They may be rushing the process. They are trying to demonstrate their independence and maturity by doing "adult" things. In reality, most of the time they're in way over their heads. They may think they're all grown up, but they're not. They're actually clueless, and hopefully they won't get hurt or hurt someone else—*including you!* They are overcompensating for their insecurity, lack of confidence, and low self-esteem.

Try to understand that although you can smoke, drink, have sex, and do all kinds of things that adults do, that doesn't make you an adult. Yes, you may be physically able to do these things but, in truth, it's absolutely impossible for any teenager to *knowingly* and comfortably swim in these deep and choppy waters. The key word is "knowingly." Yes, you can swim in the ocean, but you can swim for only so long in the middle of the ocean before you get tired, make a mistake, and get into trouble. Your instinct may be to jump right in and test the deep water. *Don't do it.*

You'll have more confidence if you start a little slower and build your understanding and strength. Allow yourself time to grow. With each passing day, you will begin to feel better and understand more about who you are, what you want to do, and where you want to be. At the same time, you will begin to see who you're not and what you don't want to do. You will make the conscious decision to avoid people, places, and situations that put you in harm's way. You will better understand where you fit in.

As you become more aware, your confidence will grow. You will become stronger. Your thinking will develop, mature, and become clearer. Give yourself time. It's a big ocean. Stay close to the shore and work your way out slowly.

You may ask, *How does this help me right now?* Here's the answer: Knowledge is power. If you understand what's happening to you right now, you will better navigate your way through the choppy waters. If you understand that you're in transition, you're growing, that things are changing, and that this is all completely what's supposed to be happening, then you can *slow down, be more patient, be more careful, and allow yourself to evolve.*

Your confidence and self-esteem are growing with each passing day, and with each chapter you read. Hang in there. You will be just fine.

Chapter Fourteen ~

Change Your Attitude...
Change Your Life

*P*lease forgive me if I sound like I'm preaching in this chapter. I can't express strongly enough my belief that *a change in attitude will make your life so much better*. Here goes.

Attitude. We've all got it. Sometimes it's verbal. More often it's nonverbal. The trick is keeping an eye on it so that it doesn't cause us too many problems when we push the "attitude button." If we push the attitude button too often, it will come back to bite us.

Believe me, I know. I've got attitude. When I don't like something I hear, I say, "Whatever." To me, "whatever" means I hear you, but I'm not interested and I'm not listening. I usually get in big trouble when I push the "whatever" button. Nowadays, I make a serious effort to avoid saying, "Whatever." It just opens the door to trouble. Years ago, my college roommate tried to help me out. "Rick," he said, "people are like bees. If you don't mess with them, they won't sting you."

I was way too proud. When I heard this, my response was, "Whatever." Now, I've come to realize that he was absolutely right. I should have listened to him a lot sooner.

Just like me, my kids have attitude. The body language attitude seems to be the loudest. When the eyes start rolling, the conversation heats up. I don't know what it is about the rolling eyes, but if you ever want to get your parents, teachers, or friends really mad, just let 'em roll. But watch out for that body language. Those rolling eyes might bite you.

Sometimes you might get into trouble with your parents, and you have absolutely no idea why. It could be because you gave attitude earlier and your parents are getting mad about it much later. Last night, you rolled your eyes or jumped at them when they said something. Watch out. It doesn't take much to trigger the delayed consequences of attitude. The next morning, your parents might bite your head off for no apparent reason. The consequences of attitude can bite you long after the attitude button was pushed.

The thing about attitude is understanding why it happens. Often you give attitude when you're tired or you disagree with something you see or hear, or you think what's being said or asked of you is *not important*. What you may not understand is that the people you're giving attitude to are probably thinking almost *the exact same* thing, but from their own point of view.

They, too, are tired. They disagree with something they see or hear, but to them, what they're saying or asking *is very important*. For example, your parents want you to do something NOW, but you don't think it's important, so you give attitude. The gap between "not important" versus "very important" is often where attitude kicks in. The same "important" versus "not important" gap exists when you give attitude to your teachers or friends.

Another attitude trigger happens when someone offers you help, but you don't think you need the help. So you decide to be rebellious. My advice is, *don't be defiant to make a point.* In fact, don't be stubborn or defiant at all. That's another form of attitude. You made your point! *The only person you're really hurting is yourself. What good was that?* Don't make the same mistake I made with my roommate. We all need help.

Don't let pride blind you. Don't get angry and defensive with people who love you and are trying to help you. Give them a chance. If you don't, *they may decide to not bother helping you next time.* You can be the most beautiful girl in the world, but if you've got attitude, you may find yourself all alone. Remember, it's OK to have different opinions. Don't let that interfere with your getting help. Embrace help; cool the attitude.

Let me help you further understand why teenagers give their parents attitude. As teenagers, you are growing to be independent. Your parents have been stuck in the nurturing mode for so long that it's hard for them to let go and realize you're getting older. At the same time, you haven't yet figured out how to handle the new independence and responsibility, and the need to pay more attention to life's details that come with getting older.

You're both right. You are getting older and more capable. And, yes, along with that comes more responsibility and the need to pay attention to the details. Remember, the small detail that may not seem very important to you is probably much more important than you realize. Attention to details is the difference between an A or a B in school. It's the same in life.

Unfortunately, there are way too many details in life. When I was young, I used to hear, "The devil is in the details." I wasn't sure what it meant then, but now I know it's true. When we don't pay attention to the details, life doesn't go so well. Always make a point to pay attention to life's details—both you and your parents will appreciate your doing so.

Another thing about attitude: Be very careful when you joke with people. There's always a little truth to every joke. You know when you make a joke that is partially serious, or when you are being sarcastic. People who know better won't think your joke is funny. If you see or hear something you don't agree with, speak up. Your intelligent thoughts and suggestions are far more valuable than your sarcasm. People can learn from you just as much as you can learn from them.

The best way to deal with attitude is just to watch it. Know when you're giving it. Understand what you and the other person are both missing when attitude kicks in. Always try to understand why the issue is so important to the other person. Really try to understand where they are coming from. You may be surprised at what you learn.

The simplest way to control attitude is to think before you speak or react. Try not to jump to conclusions. Try not to be defiant. Always be open to the *possibility* that you might be wrong. I'm not saying that you are wrong; just be open to that *possibility*. I believe that the smartest people are those who realize they don't know everything. When they figure that out, they become more open-minded and more aware of what's actually going on around them.

It's true—the world does not revolve around you or me. Change your attitude, and you will change your life.

Chapter Fifteen ～

Why Do I Feel So Bad?

There will be days when you wake up and feel unhappy for absolutely no known reason. The sun is out, the sky is blue, and you can't figure out what's wrong with you. One minute you're happy, the next minute you're agitated and upset. You ask, *Am I depressed? Am I anxious? Am I going crazy? What's going on?*

Please remember: It's perfectly normal to feel down, anxious, and out of sorts for absolutely no apparent reason. Now you know you're in transition, and your body and mind are changing and growing rapidly. You are experiencing and learning so many things, so fast, that frequently life becomes overwhelming.

You are becoming more aware of the world around you. You realize that life and relationships are becoming more complicated. Your confidence and inner strength are still developing. You are processing and filtering so many things, and it's sometimes difficult to keep up. Between school, family, friends, illness, death, loss, divorce, money, and unrealistic expectations, you are on overload.

Before you jump to the conclusion that something is wrong with you, reevaluate your physical activity and your diet. There are a number of strategies to help you get through the "bad days." Let's look at a few:

Eat right: Limit sugar, fat, coffee, caffeine, soda, diet soda, and junk food. These foods, in particular, cause anxiety, irritability, and mood swings.

Exercise: Get your body moving and your blood flowing. Go for a walk, or run, dance, swim, jump rope, do some old-fashioned jumping jacks, throw in a few push-ups and sit-ups. Keep your body active and you will feel and look better. Don't sit around and do nothing. Get up, get out, and get going. Have a daily exercise routine. You will feel better almost immediately.

Stay busy: If you have too much time on your hands, you might find yourself dwelling on issues and concerns. The more free time you have, the more your mind spins and creates problems. The best way to address this is to stay busy. Get involved in school and activities that you enjoy. Spend time with people who make you happy. Listen to music that makes you dance and sing. Rent a funny movie. Go visit a friend or family member who you haven't seen for a while. Think about someone you love and write a list of all the reasons you love that person. Then call that person and read him or her your list.

Talk: Talk to people you trust. Talk to people you love. Talk to God. Pray and ask God to *help you help yourself.* Keep praying.

Use your senses: Really open your eyes and see all the beautiful things this world has to offer. See all the colors. Hear all the sounds. Smell a rose. Open up and just fill up with all that's around. Be thankful for the small things in life. Say thank you and be thankful for every day, for everybody, and for everything. Make a list of all the things you are grateful for. As you write your list, keep in mind that the best things in life are free, and the most important *things* in life are not things.

Avoid drugs and alcohol: Alcohol fills your body with empty calories and is a depressant. Drugs and alcohol chemically alter your state of mind and can make you unhappy.

Sleep: If you're tired, try to take a nap and get more sleep. You're working hard and your body is changing fast. There's a lot going on. Sleep deprivation can be a big problem at home, at school, and especially on the road if you're driving. It's OK to take a break and rest.

Try these things and I know you'll feel better. If you do all of the above and you still feel out of sorts, speak with your parents, counselor, or doctor. I strongly urge you to avoid antidepressants unless your doctor recommends otherwise for a specific medical condition. If you're able, try to find natural ways to be happy.

One last thought: Keep in mind that no matter how bad things get, you can never fall off the floor—everything will be OK.

Chapter Sixteen ~

What Do Boys Really Think About Who You Are?

I recently had a conversation with a group of high school boys, and I was very surprised to hear their thoughts regarding the actions of many of the girls in their schools.

They told me that what some girls do in high school is often very surprising and unexpected. I heard about parties where the girls sneaked in the liquor, wore very little clothing, were promiscuous, and did things and acted in ways that the boys never expected. I heard about girls who were the aggressors and put sexual demands on the boys.

The boys told me they had higher expectations of the girls than the girls actually had of themselves. When I asked them to explain further, they said they never expected the girls to be so careless (care less). They didn't really understand why the girls were the ones drinking the hard liquor, and cheapening themselves with what they wore (or didn't wear) and by what they said and how they acted.

I questioned the double standard. Why can't the girls drink hard liquor if it's OK for the boys to drink the beer? To them, the hard liquor seemed to be more of a problem. I asked why it was OK for the boys to hit on the girls and not vice versa. They said it was fine either way, but they just didn't expect the girls to be so aggressive.

The boys told me stories about different parties. The "lingerie" party seemed to be the one most on their minds. Both boys and girls throw lingerie parties where the girls dress, and sometimes act, as sexy, slutty, revealing, and promiscuous as possible. The boys had conflicting thoughts about this party.

On the one hand, the boys explained that they didn't mind how the girls were acting, and they all commented on how they enjoyed the "free show" at the lingerie party. At the same time, the boys were actually disappointed by the behavior of some of their classmates who not only made the decision to attend but went "well beyond" just being the show.

I questioned the boys' decision to attend the party in the first place. I asked them if they were the boys participating in any of the questionable "well-beyond" conduct that happened at these parties. They said they were only there to watch the "show." I asked if *all* the girls attended these parties and acted this way. They said that it was just the ones who made the decision to be there.

I asked them about the girls who decided not to attend. They actually thought much more highly of those girls. They had far more respect for the girls who made the better decisions.

I then started to hear the labels girls were given who did attend and had acted in these careless, aggressive, suggestive, and promiscuous ways. I was now very upset to hear the words the boys used to describe these girls: slut, whore, cunt, ho, cocksucker, skank, bitch, make-out whore, hand-job ho, closet whore. I'm embarrassed to even type these words, but the teenage girls previewing this book *insisted* that they be included.

These are not pretty words. They are labels that no girl would ever want to have attached to her name and reputation. The words used are certainly offensive, and these boys formed very definite opinions.

The boys told me that *they take these words very seriously.* It doesn't matter if boys are saying them to each other or directly to a girl. Although girls may think boys are joking, *they're not!* Boys also didn't have respect for girls who used those words toward each other. Not funny. One boy said, "How do you expect us to treat girls with respect when they use those words toward each other, and *they have no respect for themselves?*"

The point is, stop calling each other those words. If ever you hear any of those words being directed toward you by boys *or girls*, you should take that very seriously. It's your reputation. It's no joke. If you don't like it, tell your friends to knock it off. If you allow it to continue, those words just may stick!

If you ever hear a boy joke with you in a suggestive or sexual way, you should stop and take a very serious look at what you said or did that led to that joke. *Really think about it. Don't take it lightly or think it's funny. Tell him you don't like it and you want him to stop.* Stop it *before* it becomes a problem for you. Keep in mind that most boys won't joke like that unless you did first. If you did open the door for their jokes, please be more careful. Your joking and playfulness—if interpreted as hinting and flirting in a sexual way—can become a serious problem, *starting with* the sexual joke coming back at you. That joke is a red flag. If, on the other hand, the boys are joking like that entirely on their own, be very watchful and cautious of those boys because there is some truth in every joke.

It's perfectly OK if you get together with your *girl* friends at a party or a sorority event and you decide to dress up, or dress down, and have fun. What concerns me is when you go to *that party* with the boys and you degrade and disrespect yourself. That's crossing the line—and Halloween is no exception!

When asked, the boys all said they WILL remember the girls who attended the lingerie party in years to come. They WILL remember who they were, what they said and did, and how they acted. They also said they WILL remember the girls who didn't do these things, made the better decisions, and chose not to attend.

Lastly, the boys wanted me to let you know that they don't like that some girls who are book smart "dumb themselves down" when socializing with boys. Their point is that if a girl is intelligent, she should act intelligently. The boys think a smart girl who acts smart will probably attract a better caliber guy. Dumb girl = dumb guy. Smart girl = smart guy. A quality guy actually wants to have a good conversation with you—he's actually interested in the *real* YOU!

Why does any of this matter? It's only important if you want to know what these boys thought. There were obviously other boys at the party who did a lot more than watch. I didn't bother to ask any of them what they thought. Why bother? I have no respect for them, their opinions, or their actions. Maybe they're the ones you want to avoid communication and contact with in the first place. That's up to you.

After my conversation with the boys, what upset me the most was that the girls so willingly set themselves up and allowed themselves to be looked at and treated with disrespect. Although they got what they wanted—the boys' attention—they also *earned* their label and reputation.

This is how I see it…if YOU don't believe that these labels and stereotypes apply to YOU, then please hold yourself to a higher standard and act in a way that earns you the respect to which you are most definitely entitled. Make good choices about where you go, what you do, what you say, and how you present yourself. Represent who you are.

Chapter Seventeen ~

Don't Dress or Act Like a Ho

If you're not a ho, don't dress or act like a ho. You may ask, *What kind of rule is this?* You may say, *That's too blunt!* You're right, but what's not to understand about this rule? Let me ask you a few questions. Do you dress one way when you leave home and end up wearing something totally different when you get where you're going? Why on earth would you want to present yourself to the world dressed or acting like a slut? Why would you ever lower your standards and your dignity by allowing yourself to be looked at like the "show" at a lingerie theme party? Do you really want that kind of attention?

You might think, *I'm just having fun, it's no big deal.* **The reality is that it IS a big deal when you portray yourself as something you are *NOT*.**

You need to understand *how* boys evaluate you. Whether it's true or not, what you say and how you dress and act tells boys the following things about you: how you see yourself, how you want them to see and think about you, and how you want to be treated. They think they can tell if you are willing to be promiscuous. They believe that how you dress says how aggressively you want them to approach you, how far they can go with you, and how willing you are to do careless things. The more suggestive your attire, words, and actions, the more aggressive the response, and the less respect you get.

If you want this kind of attention, then dress and act the part, but you'd better be prepared for the attention, the consequences, and the reputation that will follow you in years to come. It's one thing to be looked at with disrespect, if that's how you want yourself to be seen and be remembered. It's an entirely different thing when you set yourself up to be treated and handled that way. You are so much more than a mere object or piece of meat for the viewing pleasure of boys. Don't allow yourself to be seen that way. Act and dress as you wish to be treated and respected.

Please keep in mind that there is a very fine line between flirting and being a tease. *You know when you're crossing the line by hinting and flirting in a sexual way.* Watch yourself—the boys on the receiving end can easily interpret your words and actions as an invitation. Although YOU know that you don't have to be romantic to be friends with boys, boys absolutely DON'T know this—*especially when you hint, flirt, tease or mislead! You don't have to do very much.* Something as simple as dancing suggestively can cause you more problems than you realize.

The boys will often think that you are coming on to them and that they want them to do the same. They will tease back and sometimes *joke with you in a similar way,* right then or later, following up on what you said or in response to how you acted. *But they're not joking.* They will look for the first opportunity to act on your hints and flirting. They are more than willing to give you what they *think* you are asking for. After all, *you set yourself up!* You opened up the door by flirting.

Please be very careful what you want or ask for—you just might get it. It is so easy to let down your guard. If you're in the wrong place at the wrong time, with the wrong person, you might find yourself in the uncomfortable position of being asked to or actually doing something you absolutely don't want to do. You may not know what to say. You may not know how to stop. What do you do then? You have two choices—finish what you started with your flirting and live with the consequences, or *say no and get up and leave*. Which will you pick? Either way, you've put yourself in a bad situation. If you make the wrong decision, you lose. **The point is, don't start something you don't intend to finish. Don't flirt if you don't intend to follow through!**

I'm not telling you how to act, what to say, or what to wear. It's perfectly OK to dress up and look beautiful. It's perfectly OK to be friends with boys. And it's okay if you kiss a boy. The problem starts when you kiss *so many boys* that they start *comparing notes and talking smack* about YOU! How many boys do you think you can kiss before the comparisons start and the bad reputation kicks in? Once again, I'm talking about crossing the line. I want you to realize that *it's a very fine line, and the line is too easy to cross*. Don't give the boys *or girls* something to say about YOU.

I want you to know that people will respond to you throughout your life by how you dress, what you say, and how you act. Think about the impression you want to make, and how you want to be perceived before you say and do something. Think before you put it on or take it off. Think before you go to a particular party with a particular theme. Think before you hint, flirt, tease, randomly make-out or hook-up with the hot jerk or any boy. What message are you communicating? Will you be respected? Just think about who you are!

Do the math. The attention you want + the recognition you get = the label you're given and the reputation that follows you throughout life! The answer can be either a positive or a negative depending entirely on the type of *attention* YOU want.

Chapter Eighteen ~

Respect Yourself

Always respect yourself and your body. Why? Because you're given only one life and only one body.

Ask yourself these questions before you consider any questionable activity:

1. Am I respecting myself by doing...
2. Am I maintaining my dignity by doing...
3. Am I respecting the people I love by doing...
4. Am I getting any real benefit by doing...
5. Can I hurt myself by doing...
6. Can I hurt the people I love by doing...
7. How serious are the consequences of my doing...
8. Am I making a choice consistent with my values by doing...
9. What is the long-term effect of my doing...
10. Will I change my future by doing...
11. How will I be remembered if I do this?

Think long and hard about your answers to these questions. Your answers will help you make the right decisions. *But be very careful.* **Don't let your mind trick you into ignoring your an-**

swers to these questions and lead you into making the wrong decision.

If I were to summarize this entire book in just one word, that word would be "respect." Everything you do and everything you say comes down to respect. *Each and every situation I address in this book is simply an example of respect.* **Always respect yourself**.

If you respect yourself, people will respect who you are. If you don't, they won't.

Your Parents

You Didn't Enter This World with a How-To Manual   65

I Don't Like My Parents' Behavior   67

Stereotypes   69

Just Do Your Best   71

Pick Your Fights   73

How to Tell Your Parents   75

Chapter Nineteen ~

You Didn't Enter This World With a How-To Manual

When you were born, you didn't come with a manual. For a parent, a manual would be very handy.

We, as parents, don't always know the right answer. We don't always know when you should or shouldn't be allowed to go out or do certain things. We're not always sure how late you should stay out. In most circumstances, your parents are doing their very best to raise you the right way and to teach you right from wrong. But we need help from you.

If you see things happening at home that you disagree with, please help us out. *Consider being the adult that you want your parents to be.* Try to stay calm, focused, and take the initiative. Talk to us. Keep talking to us. Sometimes we can be stubborn. Sometimes we don't listen as well as we should. Sometimes we jump to conclusions. Sometimes we need help, too. Don't give up on us.

Try to explain to us what you want us to know. Use your words and communication skills. Make your point clear. Speak with authority. Don't whine or pout. It will get you absolutely nowhere. *Use the approach and tone of voice that you want us to use when we speak with you.* Don't expect immediate results but keep in mind that the more you use this approach, the sooner we will understand and respect your words and thoughts.

If you have a hard time talking, write us a letter or send us an email. Writing is a less confrontational way for you to get your message across to us. It also gives us time to think about what you're saying. Hopefully your parents will begin to understand and come around; if by chance they don't, be resourceful—talk to other people you trust.

In a perfect world, both parent and child learn from each other. But our world is far from perfect. Help your parents be as good as they can be. As soon as you stop talking to your parents and the people you trust, the more likely you are to encounter problems.

Your voice is our "how-to" manual.

Chapter Twenty ~

I Don't Like My Parents' Behavior

"**M**y parents are driving me crazy! They just don't get it. I don't like what they say or do, how they look, or how they act. It's embarrassing."

It's difficult when you actually realize that your parents are not perfect. They say and do things that you absolutely don't agree with. They embarrass you. They may be hypocrites who don't practice what they preach. At times, you feel that everything they do and say is wrong.

I'm not here to defend your parents but simply to confirm what you may have already come to realize. Your parents are not perfect.

You may want to change or improve them but don't be disappointed if that doesn't happen. Instead, learn from them and their mistakes and *improve yourself.* You are absolutely not destined to repeat your parents' mistakes.

Learn the things that you don't like about your parents and make a point not to carry those traits forward with you in your own life. Make a point not to make the same mistakes as your parents. At the same time, learn and appreciate the fine qualities that your parents do have. Cherish those qualities and make those positive aspects part of your life.

Accept and love your parents for who they are. Learn from your parents, but don't repeat their mistakes.

Chapter Twenty-one ~

Stereotypes

You are a person who is entitled to respect. Your culture, religion, upbringing, ethics, and morals are woven into the fabric of who you are. The people sitting next to you all have stories, some similar, many different. The stories of their lives create the people they are.

Everyone has a story. Every person is entitled to respect before you judge him or her, apply stereotypical thinking, have negative impressions, and draw negative conclusions. To do so is being naïve and closed-minded. We come from different places, speak different languages, and have different religions, cultures and life-styles, but we often share much more in common than we realize.

Be open-minded about different people, cultures, religions, and lifestyles. I'm simply asking you to not prejudge people based on a stereotype before you've had a chance to find out their stories and who they are.

Never, and I mean *never*, think that you are better than other people. Just because your skin color is different from theirs, or you may have more opportunities, more privileges, more money, nicer clothes, a better education, a better job, and/or a bigger house, doesn't mean that you are better than any other person. *Every person has something to teach you.* You are no better than anyone else!

It's not uncommon for parents to have stereotypes about different races, religions, cultures, sexual orientations, occupations, political parties, and various other issues. Their opinions are the result of life experiences *they* have had, where they grew up, and how they were raised. Remember, these are your parents' experiences, not necessarily yours. Give yourself time to develop your own opinions and beliefs.

Listen closely to what your parents say and try to understand the story that led them to their opinions. At the same time, don't blindly adopt your parents' prejudices and stereotypes. Try to be more open-minded. Allow yourself to be open to the possibility that your parents might be wrong.

You have the ability to evaluate people as individuals. Treat and respect people as you would expect them to treat and respect you.

Chapter Twenty-two ~

Just Do Your Best

You absolutely do NOT have to be perfect! Just do your very best.

It's impossible to be perfect. There's no such thing. There's no one definition of "perfect." Is it the body? Is it the money or clothes? Is it the brains? Is it the implants? Is it the fake tan? Is it the make-up? *Is it Photoshop?* Which one? What combination? Who knows?

Are TV and magazine models perfect? The reality is that no matter who you are, you don't look so great when you first wake up in the morning. Think about it. No one is perfect.

Each one of us is given a gift and/or a talent in life. We all excel in different things. Sometimes our peers are better than us at certain things, and at times, we excel to a higher level in our own realms. That's just the way it goes.

Always remember that YOU are unique. Be true to yourself. Go with what you've got. Make the most of it. Set your own expectations of yourself. Set them as high as you know you are capable of reaching, but be realistic. Don't set your expectations so high that you never meet them; if you do, you are setting yourself up for failure and disappointment. Reevaluate and adjust your expectations often, always keeping your goals in mind.

Let me ask: Are your parents' high expectations causing you a problem? Do they want you to have better grades, get into a more prestigious college, or have a higher paying job? If so, make a point to tell them you disagree. Help them understand. Let them know how you feel and how their expectations are hurting you. Don't make yourself sick trying to meet your parents' unrealistic expectations. It's perfectly fine to expect and want more from yourself. Just don't go overboard. Slow down. Work smart. Work hard. Take small steps and better yourself with each passing day.

The only thing that matters is that YOU know in your mind and in your heart that you have always done your very best at whatever you are trying to accomplish.

Chapter Twenty-three ~

Pick Your Fights

*H*ere's the conflict: Parents want what's best for their kids, but many times what's best is not always what kids want. What do you do? Here's the answer: *Pick your fights, and try to use effective communication skills.*

The next time your parents say "NO" to something you want to do, try a new strategy.

Step 1: Ask yourself, *Is what I'm asking really important—going to a movie, a sleepover, or just hanging out with friends?* If not, *let it go this time*; it's not worth the fight. Don't give attitude. Don't go into attack mode. Stay calm. Say the following: "You're right, Mom, this one's not so important. But, please, at least think about it the next time I ask if I can do something that *is* more important."

You have just handled yourself in a mature and articulate manner, and you have demonstrated that you are capable of having an intelligent discussion. Whether they show it or not, your parents will be impressed. Keep this up. They will begin to give you more freedom when you show them that you are articulate, capable, and mature. When you act this way, you are beginning to teach your parents how to be a little more open-minded and accepting of you, your abilities, and your thoughts. The better you communicate and the more mature you act and are, the better your relationship will be with your parents and the more success you will have with Steps 2 and 3.

Step 2: If what you're asking is really important—the prom or a big event— try saying the following words:

"Mom, I really want you to *consider* what I'm asking. This is important to me for the following reasons...Is there some way we can compromise so that we can both be happy?" This approach may just work. *It's far more effective than whining and pouting.* Say what's on your mind in a calm and intelligent way.

Step 3: If you're still getting nowhere, try my older daughter's strategy. In ninth grade, she wanted to go out and hang with friends. Her mom and I weren't too happy about the time and place, and we told her we had to think about it. She said, "Dad, please don't think too long, because I really want your permission. I don't want to sneak behind your back. I don't want to lie to you." I appreciated her approach. I didn't want her to lie to me either. The next day, we compromised, and we both got what we wanted. Try her strategy; it may work for you, too.

Using your communication skills will get you a lot further than giving attitude and being stubborn and defiant.

More attitude + more defiance = less getting what you want.

Use your words. Even if it doesn't work at first, keep trying. The better you communicate, the more likely you will get what you want and the better relationship you will have with your parents.

Pick your fights.

Chapter Twenty-four ~

How to Tell Your Parents

I understand that we do not all have parents who are alive or who may be living with us. You may be living with family, friends, or others who are your primary caregivers and source of support. When I refer to parents in this chapter, I am including all of your caregivers.

One of the most difficult things to do is to tell your parents you made a mistake. This chapter will help you out. Before I give you my thoughts, I want to tell you a little about how your parents think. This will help you better understand how to tell your parents *anything*. By the way, when I say the "bullet," I'm referring to whatever it is that hurts you.

Your parents' three biggest fears for you are that: 1) the "bullet" will hit you, 2) they were not there and were not able to stop the bullet, and 3) you will not let them help you recover from the bullet.

Let me help you better understand your parents.

First, no true parent ever wants you to get hurt in any way. It really doesn't matter what the bullet is; the fact that you got hurt is painful to a parent. I understand that there are different levels of getting hurt including being excluded, being manipulated, getting drunk and getting sick, having sex that you now regret, getting pregnant, having an abortion. The fact that *anything* unexpected and hurtful has happened to you is painful to your parents.

Your parents were teenagers, too. It may not seem like it, but it really wasn't that long ago. Your parents know what it feels like to get hurt. They know what it's like to make mistakes. They remember their own mistakes and the mistakes of their friends. Their eyes have seen a lot more than you can ever imagine. They have seen and felt the pain of the bullet in their own lives. They have made mistakes that you will never know about. They really do understand and feel your pain. When they are raising you, they do *everything* in their power to protect you from being hurt and from making the same mistakes. That's why they're so scared that the "bullet" will hit you.

Second, your parents fear that they will not be there to stop you from getting hurt, or somehow they were not able to stop what happened. They will blame themselves for not teaching you how to better protect yourself, for allowing you to go to where you got hurt, or for not taking the time to watch you more closely. It all comes down to the fact that your parents were unable to somehow prevent the pain, even if there was absolutely nothing they could have done to stop what happened. They couldn't stop the bullet.

Third, your parents fear that you will not let them help you recover from the bullet. They're scared you won't let them in. You won't tell them what happened. They can't help you recover. When your parents know something is wrong with you, there is nothing worse for them than your not letting them in to help.

In summary, your parents' thinking is that you got hurt, and they didn't or couldn't stop it. Now they're not there to help you get through it.

From your point of view, you may not want to tell your parents what happened. You don't want to hurt or disappoint them. You don't want them to get mad or upset. You don't know what they'll say and how they'll respond. Will they ground you? Will they think less of you? Will they understand what happened? Do they even know how to help you? Will telling them just cause more problems?

You have mixed emotions. On the one hand, you want to tell them everything just to get it all out. You don't want to lie anymore. You want them to help you better understand what happened and why. You want them to help you make it better. On the other hand, you're hurt and angry because you don't think you can talk to them. They don't get it. You have no idea what to say or how to say it, and you're unsure if they even know how to help.

Let me try to help. I truly believe that in most situations your parents can help, and it IS better to speak with at least one parent about the bullet. If you decide to speak with only one parent, pick the parent with whom you feel you can best communicate. Ask for or pick a quiet time when you have your parent's undivided attention. Then use the following monologue to approach your parent in a way that will get you the best possible results:

"Dad, I really need to talk to you. This is really important and I want you to take some time with me. This is not easy for me to say. It's been bothering me for too long. Please don't get mad at me. Please just listen and let me get it all out. I don't want my friends' help. I want and need your help. Please don't interrupt me. Please wait a minute until after I stop talking before you say anything to me. Please just listen and try to understand. I'm sorry. I made a mistake. This is what happened…"

READ THE ABOVE PARAGRAPH TO YOUR PARENTS IF NECESSARY. It's hard for parents to ignore their child if you approach them this way. Your parents will very quickly get over their initial reactions. You have prepared them for what you have to say. By using the monologue, you are helping your parents to better help you. You're also helping them to be better parents. They will get over the initial disappointment and will begin the process of helping you to heal. I believe they will be there for you.

When you talk to your parents, be honest. Don't water down the story. Never shift the blame or responsibility. Don't accuse someone else of your thoughts and your actions. Accept *full* responsibility for what happened and what you did. Tell them the truth. After you talk with your parents, you will have earned their trust by being honest. Dishonesty destroys trust. Being honest takes courage; it's so much easier to lie.

It won't be easy, but you'll feel better knowing that you got it all out. You will have the help you need from the people who know you best—your parents. You and your parents will grow together. They can help you better understand what happened and how to make it better. You will no longer have to keep it bottled up inside and live with a lie. You will have calmed *their* fears. You will have calmed *your* fears and eased your mind. You will begin to build the foundation of trust and honesty that you truly want to have with your parents.

You and your parents will be closer if you allow them to help you. It's never too late to talk to your parents. When you do, they may soon become your best friends.

I have one final thought: If you *really* need to prepare your parents for what you have to say, consider leaving this book on the kitchen table or in the family room with a bookmark in *this* chapter. Your parents will read the chapter, get the message, and have time to prepare themselves for what you have to say. They may even approach you when *they're* ready. If they don't approach you, then after a few days, use the monologue and communicate.

You can do it. It will be OK.

How To Handle Yourself

Trust Your Stomach 83

The Most Important Word in the Dictionary is "NO" 85

Always Have a Game Plan 87

Get Up and Leave 93

Let's Teach You How to Drink 97

Watch Your Back 101

Unwanted Attention 103

Gossip 107

Disrespectful Boys/Girls and Boyfriends 109

Easy or Hard 111

Chapter Twenty-five ~

Trust Your Stomach

*E*very day you will make choices and decisions, some big and some small. It's not easy to always know what the right decision is. Usually, you do know right from wrong; other times, the decision seems more complicated, and you dwell on what to do or not to do.

My decision-making rule is simple: *Trust your stomach.* If your stomach doesn't feel well, then you know what decision you should make. *Never disregard that upset feeling in your stomach caused by caution or concern. It's your body's way of telling you that something is wrong.* No matter how long you think about a decision, your stomach will never lie. Use your stomach to help you *anticipate and avoid* people, places, and situations that can cause you problems.

While it would be nice to rely on your mind, as a teenager your stomach is a much better measuring tool. Why? Because you can *think yourself into any decision* if you rely solely on your mind. It's like having the devil on one shoulder and an angel on the other—each whispering the opposite point of view in your ears. Who do you listen to? What will you decide? The longer you dwell on an issue and go back and forth, the more likely the devil will get what he wants. The more you question and doubt yourself, the more confused you will become and the more likely you will talk yourself into making the wrong choice.

Your mind, along with your youth, your curiosity, and your confusion will often lead you to make the wrong decision. Your unsettled stomach, on the other hand, cannot be ignored.

Trust your stomach.

Chapter Twenty-Six ~

The Most Important Word in the Dictionary is "NO"

I don't know why, but saying *no* is difficult. I understand that it's hard to do, but you have to learn how to say *no*.

In high school and college, there's so much going on, and you want to do everything! The problem is, you just can't. If you spread yourself too thin, you'll do a lot more, but you'll accomplish a lot less. Pace yourself—say *no* sometimes.

Another thing: When your stomach tells you that something isn't right, *no* should be the first word you think of when you're unsure of the right answer—you can never go wrong by saying *no*—especially when you're saying *no* to issues like sex, alcohol and drugs.

It's never too late to say *no*. Say it loud. Repeat it. Mean it. Say *no* before it's too late to stop something bad from happening to you or to someone else. The easiest way to protect yourself is to just say *no*.

It may sound funny, but I want you to practice saying *no* in the mirror before you go to a party or before you do something you're unsure of. Look in the mirror. Watch and listen to yourself saying *no*. It's actually very difficult. In fact, try it right now. Come on. Try it just once! If you can't say *no* to yourself in the mirror, then how do you expect to say it to someone else?

No matter how much you practice, saying *no* is still hard. If you find yourself unable to say *no*, try this strategy: Blame your parents. That's right. It's perfectly OK to say, "My parents won't let me," or "My mom's a bitch; she wants me home NOW." Even if you have to pretend on the phone that a parent is giving you a hard time, if this is what you need to do to get out of a situation or to say *no*, go for it. Another strategy is to change the subject, but this one doesn't always work so well, especially when someone is being persistent.

Use whatever strategy works best for you to get *no* across. Just remember, you absolutely have the right to say *no*. Never feel bad about saying *no*. Remember: *No will help you only if you actually say it. Leaving it unsaid leaves you vulnerable.*

I know you don't always want to say *no*. Just keep it in mind and use *no* to avoid questionable situations. This one little word will save you over and over again throughout your life.

Chapter Twenty-Seven ~

Always Have a Game Plan

I know it's often difficult to have a game plan during high school and college. Plans change quickly, and it's difficult (sometimes almost impossible) to know exactly where you're going to be and who is going to be there. It is absolutely impossible to know what will happen when you get there.

It's because of this uncertainty that you must ALWAYS have a game plan. Never *assume* that things will just work out. That's not how life works. Things rarely just work out. *Pay attention to the details.* Let me explain.

Let's say you're going out one night. What details should you think about? The first thing is to know *who* you're going with. It's always a good idea to go with a friend who is in sync with you, who will look for you at the party if five or ten minutes pass and she doesn't know where you are. Go with a friend who will never question your decision to leave immediately. Make that agreement with your friend BEFORE you go so that you are both on the same page. If either of you says, "It's time to leave," you've already decided to respect each other's decision.

Anticipate with your friend what is likely to happen when you get where you're going. Consider and talk about the possibilities *before* you go. Who will be there, what's likely to happen when you get there, and what you will and will not do when you're there. Never cross the boundaries you set. If you think you're going to have a hard time NOT crossing the line, then *absolutely don't put yourself in a bad situation.* Don't go.

Next, you must know *how* you're going to get where you're going. Is someone driving? It must be perfectly clear that whoever is driving is absolutely not drinking. That person is the designated driver.

Never forget the next and often most important detail: You must ALWAYS *plan your exit* and know how you are getting home. Don't ignore this crucial detail. You never want to be left behind—you must *always anticipate and know exactly what you will do to get out* of a situation or location. Don't make the mistake and *ASSUME* you will get a ride—think it through and plan your exit strategy long before you go! Also, NEVER get into a car alone with a boy you don't know well. Just because he goes to your school, is an acquaintance, or is a friend of a friend doesn't mean YOU know him. You are putting yourself at more risk than you realize. He can take you anywhere he wants after you get in and close that car door. Don't be so naïve. Get rides only from people you know and trust.

If you decide to leave your local area or city, pay extra attention to the details. The farther away you get from home base, the less likely you'll have access to timely help if you need it. Also, the less familiar you are with your surroundings, the more likely you are to find yourself in the wrong place at the wrong time.

Discuss your game plan with your parents before you leave. Call them often during the night to update them with changes. Also, know the plans of your family for the evening so that you know where to reach them. If your plans change, alert one another. Communicate with your parents throughout the night.

By the way, if you choose to lie about where you are or what you're doing, still check in. Lying is a bad idea. Lying and not checking in is even worse. Call home. You never know when you might need help. And never leave the house without your charged cell phone and enough money to catch a cab or public transportation.

If you're at a sleepover and you decide to sneak out at night, please think twice before doing so. Balance the risk of sneaking out versus the adventure. Never go out alone. Again, never go too far from home base. The problem with sneaking out is that no one knows you're gone. If you need help, it may be several hours before someone realizes you are missing. That's an awful lot of time to pass if you need help. Again, take your cell phone and make sure it's fully charged. A call for help is much less of a problem than the consequences of finding yourself once again in the wrong place at the wrong time.

Curfew Tips: If you have a curfew, try to **get home ten minutes** *early*. Your parents *will* notice you're acting responsibly. Also, make a point to call your parents *throughout the night* **and before** they call you. Your parents will appreciate your making a point to call. If something comes up and you're going to be late, call home at least thirty minutes *before* curfew to let your parents know you're running late. Keep checking in soon after you're late to update them on your status and how soon you'll be home. The better you communicate and handle curfew, the more you establish trust. The more you check in and communicate, the fewer problems you'll have, even if you get home past curfew.

Think about it. The fact that you have a curfew at all shows your parents' love and concern. In fact, all your parents' rules are for the sole purpose of keeping you safe. They may seem strict, but they're intended to protect you and keep you out of harm's way. When you ignore and disrespect these rules, including your curfew, you show them you don't care. At the same time, you are putting yourself at risk. The risk is very real. Once again, you have a decision to make. Do you lie and sneak around, or do you follow the rules that your parents hope and pray will protect you? It's your life. It's your call.

Fake ID's: If you decide to get or use a fake ID, realize you are doing so at your own risk. If you use a fake ID that's in your name, authorities can charge and prosecute you. If you use another person's ID, you risk even greater consequences, including prosecution for identity theft. But there are *far greater dangers* when you use a fake ID.

If you use a fake ID to get into an adult venue, including a bar or a club, you will likely find yourself in the company of adult men, not boys. Men in bars are calculating, aggressive, persuasive, and they have high expectations of you. Those men could include sexual offenders and sexual predators looking and waiting for someone *just like you. They figure that if you're willing to play the game by being there, then you're willing to pay the price!* How willing are you? ***Please* don't ignore what happened to these girls**:

- What was supposed to be a night of fun ended in tragedy. Eighteen-year-old Jennifer Moore was kidnapped, beaten, sexually assaulted and killed after she sneaked into a club and drank heavily.[5]
- A 17-year-old girl allegedly was gang-raped in a basement apartment by three young men who met her inside a popular club. The underage girl told cops she sneaked into the club where she drank inside the nightspot. Apparently, she left the club, passed out and woke up as she was being raped.[6]
- Natalee Ann Holloway disappeared during an unofficial high school senior class graduation trip in Aruba. Holloway remains officially missing to this day, although according to Aruban authorities, she is most likely dead. She was last seen leaving the vicinity of a popular tourist-oriented bar with three men.[7]

These girls were all underage, were in the wrong place with the wrong people, and paid the price—none of them wanted or expected these things to happen. There are countless incidents of minors and even a *dult women* who have similar stories after going out on the town and hitting the clubs. Please take this seriously. Don't be foolish and use a fake ID or go places where you don't belong.

Finally, *please* never lie about where you are spending the night. If you have to lie about where you're sleeping, ***the opportunities to make a serious mistake are endless.***

I trust my children. It's everyone and everything around them that causes me the greatest concern for their safety and well-being. We are all vulnerable and susceptible to making mistakes. *None of us is immune to temptation and harm.* It will be that way every day of our lives. That's why it's so important for you to *anticipate and avoid* doing things that are foolish, dangerous, or against your better judgment.

The whole purpose of having a game plan is to anticipate and avoid people, places, situations, and environments that put you at further risk by tempting you *to be even more likely* to make a mistake that you don't want to make. You never want to put yourself in the wrong place or be with the wrong people. Without a game plan, you will make choices based on circumstances, pressures, and your mood at the moment. It's just too easy to let down your guard, and the consequences of doing so can be devastating.

After reading this chapter, I want you to take a minute and really think about your answers to the following three questions. *How many of these strategies will I actually use?* If you decide to disregard *any* of the strategies, then ask and answer, *Why am I allowing myself to be so vulnerable? Why am I so willing to deliberately risk my physical safety?*

Now you know the rules of the game. It's totally up to you to decide whether or not to apply them.

Chapter Twenty-Eight ~

Get Up and Leave

*I*t is inevitable that, at some point in time, you will find yourself somewhere you don't want to be or doing something you don't want to do.

It may be a moment in time when you're beginning to take steps you truly don't want to take. You can be anywhere, with anyone, and you know that something's not right. You may be about to get into a car you know you should not get into or about to go somewhere you know you should not go. You may be about to have sex, drink, smoke a joint or do cocaine. Whatever it is, you realize you are about to do something that you question, or something that doesn't pass the stomach test.

What do you do at that moment? You have to make a choice. It may sound hard to do, but if you don't like what's about to happen, the rule is very simple: *Just get up and leave, right then and there.* Don't worry about what other people think if you make the decision to get up and leave. Say out loud or to yourself, *I'm out of here,* and leave.

You just made that decision for the right reasons. What was happening no longer passed the stomach test. Act on your decision to leave right then and there. Don't wait. Don't open or walk through a door that you're not ready for. If you somehow do go through that door and you realize you don't belong there, STOP! Get up and leave.

What if you don't have a way to get to a safe place? Call home, a friend, a friend's parent, or even the police. If you don't need to call or don't have time to call, then just *walk away* from the situation and away from where you don't want to be.

Don't worry about getting into trouble by calling and asking for help. The trouble you get in will be much less of a problem than the consequences of staying someplace you really don't want to be or doing something that you truly don't want to do.

You have the absolute right to change your mind at any time. **That's right. It's your mind, your body, and your right!**

While it would have been a better idea to avoid putting yourself in that situation in the first place, it's never, never too late to change your mind.

Make a point to write down on your "Who I Am Not…" list what happened so that you avoid the situation in the future.

If by chance you did not get up and leave in time, learn from the experience. That's all that matters. Just learn the lesson. Don't allow yourself to be defined by the one mistake. If you learn the lesson, the "get up and leave" rule will be easier to follow next time. Better yet, you may learn the lesson so well that you avoid a similar situation the next time it is presented.

The reality is that similar situations *will* be presented to you again and again and again. *Every day of your life you will be tempted to make wrong choices.* Next time, you will know better how to protect yourself from the start and at every step along your decision-making process. You'll be stronger and better prepared to take care of and protect yourself.

I realize that to "get up and leave" is a lot easier said than done. But when you find yourself in an uncomfortable situation, you have a choice to make right then and there. Do you stay or go? You need to be strong enough to do what's right for you. FOR YOU! ONLY YOU!

Don't allow yourself to be caught in a bad situation. Get up and leave.

Chapter Twenty-nine ~

Let's Teach You How to Drink

If I had my way, you wouldn't drink in the first place. But since I don't always get what I want, it's important that you know how to drink if you decide to do so. That's right. You need to know *how* to drink, how much to drink, and how to handle your drink.

I'm not just talking about what's in the cup. I'm talking about the cup itself and how to handle the cup.

Never take a drink from someone you don't know, and never pour yourself a drink from the punch bowl. You don't know what's in it. Always, *always* get your own drink. At least you know what's in it.

If you go to a party and leave your drink on a table, never, and I mean NEVER, drink from that cup again. You don't know what was slipped into your cup while you were away. Also, never drink from someone else's cup—you don't know what's in their drink.

Date rape often results from a girl being slipped a spiked drink; that's *any* drink that's laced with x, y, or z. The drink does not have to be alcohol. Date rape occurs in high school and on almost every college campus in this country. One very important way to protect yourself is to watch your drinks. On a side note, if you *ever* hear a boy or girl friend of yours joke in *any way* about "roofies" or rape, call him or her out! Let them know you don't think they're funny! Keep this in mind when reading the statistics in Chapter 36.

Okay, let's get back on track. If you're at a party and someone offers you a drink but you don't drink, thank the person and say you don't drink. That's your decision. If the person doesn't respect your decision, that's their problem, not yours. You should never be ashamed of your morals, decisions, or the good choices you make.

No one should feel the need to hide the fact that he or she doesn't want to drink. However, if you're not strong enough to say who you are, and you decide you need to have a drink to fit in, then simply hold the drink. If you want, take an occasional sip. Just remember that you don't actually have to drink it.

Keep in mind that it's important to be comfortable in a social setting without drinking. Don't be social only when you're drinking. If you find that you need to drink to socialize, something's wrong and needs to be changed. Don't drink if you're not comfortable with who you are when you are not drinking.

Another thing: *Watch out for boys trying to get you drunk!* Again, look at the statistics in Chapter 36. One teenage girl asked me to emphasize the following point: "Never drink or get drunk with people you don't know. You are absolutely asking for trouble if you do." My additional thought is that you should *never* get drunk with boys *even if you do know them.* You are risking a lot more than your reputation by doing so.

Keep in mind that, if you're drinking alcohol, make a point to also drink water throughout the night. It will help you to rehydrate your body and hopefully help you avoid being sick or getting alcohol poisoning. Also, add extra ice to your drink. The ice will fill your cup, water down the alcohol, and make your drink last longer. And don't forget to eat.

If you choose to drink, decide for yourself how many is too many. The more you drink, the less able you are to protect yourself. Know your limit. Don't get near or cross the line. You don't have to down that 40—it's an awfully big beer! Never take shots of alcohol (quickly drinking one drink after another), especially if boys are encouraging you to do so. *You are being set up*! That's just stupid and careless. Drink one drink at a time and wait a good long time before you have the next one.

Finally, keep an eye on fruit-flavored hard liquor which can fool you into drinking more than you realize. You don't want any of these drinks sneaking up on you. Keep track of how many drinks you've had. If you can't keep track, you've had too many. *Never* put yourself in the position of not being able to remember what you said or did. This means you may be drunker than you think!

The more you drink, the more at risk you are, and the more regrets you *will* have. Your safety and well-being are entirely in your hands. ***Don't give someone the opportunity to take advantage of you.***

You decide. It's your call.

⟋⟀

Chapter Thirty ~

Watch Your Back

You must always keep your eyes open and know how to handle yourself, even when you're doing something as simple as walking down the street.

Here's the rule: *Always be aware of everyone around you.* No need to be paranoid; just be aware.

If you're walking or jogging and a car pulls alongside of you and the driver *or passenger* appears to want to ask you for directions, don't answer; keep walking or jogging. Never lean into the car window or get near the car door. Don't worry about being rude. You're not Google Maps. Let them get directions from someone else. Be leery. Keep walking. Too many girls have been pulled into a car and kidnapped in this exact situation. This happened to a very close friend of mine in college. She barely got away.

When walking down the street, look ahead to see who is coming your way. If you don't like what you see, cross the street to the other side, *long before* you cross the person's path.

Many women, especially when they go out at night, carry a whistle on their keychain and have pepper-spray or mace in their purse, just in case they are attacked. It's no joke—these items can keep you safe and save your life!

If you walk by a group of guys who start yelling catcalls or saying something inappropriate, just keep walking and look straight ahead. Don't forget about your body language. Watch your eye contact. A glare may be an open invitation for trouble. Don't look down. Stand tall and confident. You don't want to appear scared. Don't entertain their disrespect by responding. I know that instinctively you may want to react. Don't.

Remember, being impulsive can sometimes be a problem. You never know who you just flipped off, and how he or she will respond.

Chapter Thirty-one ~

Unwanted Attention

What do you do if you are getting attention you don't want? There is a fine line between receiving unwanted attention and being stalked. In either case, you should treat these situations exactly the same. *You must stop the unwanted attention immediately.* The person giving unwanted attention could be someone you know, or someone you don't know. It doesn't matter either way. My definition of a "stalker" is *anyone* contacting you who you don't want to hear from. Anyone!

Don't feed off the attention. If you don't like the person giving that attention, make it stop. Don't delay. The longer you delay, the worse it becomes and the more likely it is that you will have problems. The less you speak up, the more attention you will get. If you try to hide or simply don't respond, you are sending the stalker the nonverbal message that you really don't mind the contact because you are not telling the person to stop. Silence can be your worst enemy. *Use your words.* Make it perfectly clear that you don't like the attention and you want it to stop NOW.

People who give unwanted attention are "thick" and sometimes calculating. That means they may not get what you are saying, or they interpret your silence as wanting them to continue trying to contact you. It also means that you need to be cautious and alert as to their true intentions. They can be unpredictable. They are often manipulative. If they continue to give you attention, knowing that you don't want it, they are acting with purpose and intent. Unwanted attention can never be taken lightly.

How do you stop unwanted attention? If you get a phone call, a text message, or an email, respond on the first occasion by telling the person that you are not interested in being contacted by them. On the second occasion, respond with one sentence: "Please stop contacting me." If you hear from the person again, this response alone will have little meaning. You must take additional steps to protect yourself and to step up your defense.

Tell your friends and the people close to you that you're getting this attention that you don't want. Let them know that it upsets you. Ask them to speak up and advocate for you. Make it perfectly clear to them that you want and need their help. Never, under any circumstances, meet the person alone.

At the same time, tell your parents, teachers, and counselors what is happening and ask an adult to call and talk to the stalker. If the advances keep coming, call the police and ask them to contact the stalker. Also call your phone carrier and have the person's number blocked or traced. If necessary, change your number.

Don't think you can stop this by yourself. Don't give the impression that you can handle it. Swallow your pride. You absolutely cannot handle this by yourself. Never try to do it alone. *Make a point to get the help you need.* Unwanted attention can be dangerous.

One last thing: Don't let anyone ever touch or grab you without your permission. Not in the halls at school or on a public street. Not at any time or any place. If it happens in a public place and you feel unsafe, leave quickly and get to a safe place. If it happens at school or at a party, speak up and make a scene. Don't be silent. *Absolutely get that person in trouble.* If you get that person in trouble, it's not likely to happen again. If you don't speak up, it's more likely to be repeated because you did not object! If they get angry with you because you spoke up, don't stress. He's just upset because he got caught. I mean it. Don't let him get away with that nonsense. Let him keep his hands to himself.

Stop unwanted attention before it becomes a serious problem.

Chapter Thirty-two ~

Gossip

Some people, especially girls, love to gossip and exaggerate. Maybe they like to hear themselves talk or they like to complain. Maybe they have nothing better to do or to say, they think it's fun, or they love drama. Whatever the reason, it's not fun if you're the victim hurt by gossip, and everyone is talking behind YOUR back about YOU!

If you're in a group and the gossip starts flying, don't immediately join in. Decide for yourself if you want to listen to who is talking and what he or she is saying. Ask yourself if you would want the person to talk that way about YOU. If not, don't join the conversation. Don't add fuel to the fire. Leave the conversation.

I've said this over and over again. What you put out in life will come back. What goes around comes back around. If you gossip, it's guaranteed that at some point the tables will turn, and YOU will be the next victim of gossip.

If you decide to listen to the conversation and you know that what you are hearing is false, speak up. Tell them they're wrong. Do the right thing. Correct the record.

Will gossip ever end? No. Some people will gossip forever. Watch what you say around girls and boys like that. You may be quoted. You may hurt someone you truly don't want to hurt. You also may be the next victim.

Try your best not to waste your time and energy on gossip. Find more important things to do with your time. You're smarter than that. There really are more interesting things to talk about.

Chapter Thirty-three ～

Disrespectful Boys/Girls and Boyfriends

*L*et's talk about disrespect. Under no circumstances should you allow any person to disrespect or lie about you. If someone says or does something negative or hurtful toward you, but it's really *not important*, then simply tell him or her to *grow up*—they are not worth your time. As a general rule, *don't waste another word or thought on that person*. However, there is an exception to this rule.

There will be times when you need to speak up to defend yourself and to **define and make clear who you are, and who you are NOT!** If you find yourself in a situation where a boy or girl says something inaccurate about something you said or did, and what he or she is saying negatively impacts your reputation, *you must speak up*, assert yourself, and make perfectly clear who you are and where you stand on the issue in question.

If what is being said about you is serious and false, then *never* remain silent, and through your silence, imply that what's being said about you is true! Where there is smoke, there is fire—if it's not true, put the fire out before it catches! *You absolutely don't want a reputation that you don't deserve!*

Let's switch gears and talk about a disrespectful boyfriend. Every couple has disagreements—that's real life—but physical or verbal abuse by either one of you toward the other is absolutely not acceptable—it goes both ways. An apology does not fix the problem! Rationalization does not mean there's not a problem. If you are in an abusive relationship, you don't need this type of person in your life. Break up and move on. If you can't, seek help to end it now. Don't allow yourself to become a victim of disrespect in an abusive relationship.

Ugly behavior in any form is *absolutely not acceptable.* If you need to, speak up, *define yourself,* defend yourself, and protect yourself.

Chapter Thirty-four ~

Easy or Hard

Bad is easy. Good is hard. Getting an F is easy. Getting an A is hard. Being late is easy. Being early is hard. Having friends is easy. Being a friend is hard. Falling is easy. Getting up is hard. Spending is easy. Saving is hard. Talking is easy. Listening is hard. Sarcasm is easy. Sincerity is hard. Lying is easy. Telling the truth is hard. Saying *yes* is easy. Saying *no* is hard. Following is easy. Leading is hard. Being unaware is easy. Being aware is hard. Missing details is easy. Paying attention to details is hard. Being irresponsible is easy. Being responsible is hard.

Doing what's right is often the hardest thing to do. Nothing in life that is worthwhile comes without effort.

Sex, Alcohol, and Drugs

Sex, Alcohol, and Drugs—Do You Need Them?   115

Statistics   117

Drugs, Alcohol, and Your Body   121

Sexual Assault, Sexual Harassment, Rape   125

The Gray Area   129

Learn the Lesson, Grieve, Forgive Yourself,
         and Move Forward   133

Chapter Thirty-five ~

Sex, Alcohol, and Drugs— Do You Need Them?

There are three things that will complicate your high school and college years, and make your teenage years more confusing than necessary—sex, alcohol, and drugs (SAD).

You don't need any of these things to have a great and fulfilling high school and college experience. In fact, each of these things can make every day of your teenage years extremely confusing, stressful, and very, very unhappy.

At first, your curiosity and natural desire to experience new things may introduce you to SAD. The problem is that your curiosity can open the door to a world you're not prepared for, and a world you probably don't want to be a part of. Never let your curiosity get the best of you and lead you astray. When you play with fire, you might get burned.

Take a minute to think about how sex, alcohol, and drugs have complicated your life and your relationships so far. For those of you who don't have too much to think about, that's great. Try to keep it that way. For so many of you, sex, alcohol, and drugs have made you sad. They have made your lives so much more difficult and complicated than necessary; they may have also hurt and affected the lives of people around you and people you love.

I know it's difficult to close a door you've opened. But we can all make our lives so much better if we simply make the choice to do so. Just take a deep breath and slow yourself down. You can keep that door closed for as long as you choose. If you *choose* to open the door to SAD, open it very slowly. If you don't like what you see, *close the door fast.*

After you read this book, you will have a better understanding of how to handle the doors to SAD. This book is intended to give you complete control of the doors you open and close in your life.

Don't get discouraged. YOU have the power to avoid and control sex, alcohol and drugs in your life. The more you become aware of the issues, the better you are able to use your words, take action, make good decisions, and apply the strategies necessary to protect yourself.

Chapter Thirty-six ~

Statistics

*H*ere are a few statistics to be aware of. According to the Core Institute, an organization that surveys college drinking practices, 300,000 of today's college students will eventually die of alcohol-related causes such as drunk-driving accidents, cirrhosis of the liver, various cancers, and heart disease. Check out these facts: [8]

- 159,000 of today's first-year college students will drop out of school next year for alcohol or other drug-related reasons;
- 90% of all campus rapes occur when alcohol has been used by either the assailant or the victim;
- As many as 70% of college students admit to having engaged in sexual activity primarily as a result of being under the influence of alcohol, or to having sex they would not have had if they had been sober;
- Female college freshmen are at the highest risk for sexual assault between the first day of school and Thanksgiving break;

- At least one out of five college students abandons safe sex practices when they're drunk;
- One night of heavy drinking can impair your ability to think abstractly for up to thirty days;
- One in twelve college males admits to having committed acts that meet the legal definition of rape or acquaintance rape;
- 55% of female students and 75% of male students involved in acquaintance rape admit to having been drinking or using drugs when the incident occurred;
- 60% of college women who are infected with *sexually transmitted infections and diseases* (STDs), including genital herpes and AIDS, report that they were under the influence of alcohol at the time they had intercourse with the infected person.

Teenage STD, Pregnancy and Rape Statistics:

- Every year, roughly nine million new sexually transmitted infections occur among teens and young adults in the United States.[9]
- Every year about one in four sexually experienced teens acquires an STD;
- In a single act of unprotected sex with an infected partner, a teenage woman has a 1% risk of acquiring HIV, a 30% risk of getting genital herpes, and a 50% chance of contracting gonorrhea.[10]
- Each year, almost one million teenage women—10% of all women aged fifteen to nineteen *and 19% of those who have had sexual intercourse—become pregnant.*[11]

- Almost *two-thirds* of all rapes were committed by someone who is known to the victim. 73% of sexual assaults were perpetrated by a non-stranger—38% of perpetrators were a friend or acquaintance of the victim, 28% were an intimate, and 7% were another relative.[12]

Rape is considered a "crime of youth," where *fifty to sixty-three percent* of reported rapes were of women under *age 18.*[13]

Don't think you're not at risk—you are!

Chapter Thirty-seven ~

Drugs, Alcohol, and Your Body

*L*et's talk about drugs, alcohol, and your body. When you make the choice to use drugs and alcohol, you are deciding to alter the delicate chemical balance of your body. You are affecting each and every vital organ that enables you to survive. You are making the decision to put your mind, body, and life at risk.

You know that drugs and alcohol impair your ability to think. Sometimes that's why you may choose to use them; you want to take a break and you don't want to think. The problem is that this logic is *seriously* flawed. Why would you ever limit and impair your ability to think and in turn, possibly not remember your actions? Your decisions won't be as sharp. You're more vulnerable to making poor choices. You're more likely to make a serious mistake that you will regret. And you put your life and the lives of other people at risk.

There are far better, healthier, and happier ways to take a break and relax. *You don't have to hurt yourself to have fun.*

You will actually have a far better time if you're more aware of what's going on around you, and you *remember* the good time you had. The fragile human body, if tampered with or pushed too far, won't work so well. There is a much darker side to drugs and alcohol than just getting a buzz or a little high. Let's take a look.

Do you want your stomach pumped? Do you want to be in a coma with the possibility of never waking up? Do you want to die of alcohol poisoning? Do you want to drown in your own vomit? You get drunk, you go to bed, and you fall asleep. You're unconscious, you vomit, and you suffocate in your own vomit. You're dead! The great guitar player Jimi Hendrix was only twenty-seven when he suffocated on his own vomit after drinking. These incidents are more common than you think.

Do you want to die from an accidental drug overdose or from drug poisoning? Singer Janis Joplin died of a heroin overdose. "Saturday Night Live" comedian Chris Farley died of an overdose of cocaine and morphine. Elvis Presley died of a heart attack brought on by an overdose of barbiturates. Anna Nicole Smith died from accidental drug poisoning after taking several different sedatives and sleeping medications along with other drugs.

What about just normal people? Nothing seems to happen to them, right?

Wrong.

Michael Duni, sixteen, was at a sleepover party supervised by a parent. When the parent went to bed, the alcohol came out. Duni had a "very high" blood alcohol level and was found dead the next morning.[14]

A fifteen-year-old Ventura, California, girl died of a possible overdose after mixing over-the-counter cold medicine with prescription drugs and alcohol.[15]

Twenty-one-year-old Meaghan Bosch, a Southern Methodist University student whose body was found in a portable toilet at a construction site, died of an accidental drug overdose. She had three types of drugs, including cocaine, in her body.[16]

You might say, "This would never happen to me...I'm not like those people."

You might remember your friends who took drugs or drank a lot and think, *This didn't happen to them, they were OK, so it won't happen to me.*

You have friends who woke up the next morning just fine. *It will wear off in the morning and everything will be OK, right?*

Be open to the possibility that you might be wrong.

What you don't realize is that you are *not* your friends. Each person's body reacts differently to different amounts of alcohol and drugs. Teenagers are *more sensitive to, and less aware of, the impairment* caused by drugs and alcohol. You may be the person with the low tolerance. YOU may be far more susceptible to risk than all of your friends. If you're lucky enough to wake up the next morning, you might be right—this time. If not, you're dead.

When you use drugs or drink alcohol, you are playing Russian roulette. Russian roulette is a tragic gun-and-bullet scenario. All the bullets are removed from a gun, except one. The bullet cylinder is spun so no one knows which shot will be deadly. The gun is put to the head and shot. If the bullet does not come out, you live. If the bullet is there, you're dead. **Absolutely never play with your life like this!**

If you want to live a long and healthy life, you must take care of your body. You know the importance of eating well and exercising. But you also need to fully understand how alcohol and drugs affect your mind and body, and how they can seriously impact and even kill you.

Appendix A of this book includes Web links for information about marijuana, LSD, ecstasy, and cocaine, including detailed information about the short- and long-term effects of these drugs on your body.

Chapter Thirty-eight

Sexual Assault, Sexual Harassment, Rape

The issues of sexual assault, sexual harassment, and rape can take up an entire book. I would like to briefly introduce you to these issues.

What is sexual assault? Sexual assault and abuse are any type of sexual activity that you do not agree to, including the following:

- Inappropriate touching
- Vaginal, anal, or oral penetration
- Sexual intercourse that you say *no* to
- Rape
- Attempted rape
- Child molestation

Sexual assault can be verbal, visual, or anything that forces a person to join in unwanted sexual contact or attention. Examples of sexual assault include exhibitionism (when someone exposes him/herself in public), incest (sexual contact between family members), and sexual harassment. Sexual assault can happen in different situations: by a stranger in an isolated place, on a public street, at school or work, on a date, or at home by someone you know.

Rape can be defined in a number of ways. One definition is that rape occurs when you are forced or *manipulated* into sexual contact, including vaginal or anal intercourse, oral sex, or penetration with a finger or an object, *without consent.* The definition is self-explanatory. Rape is a common form of sexual assault. It is committed in many situations—on a date or by a friend or an acquaintance.

Let's talk about the workplace. When you get a job, you must be especially careful to protect yourself from sexual abuse. At work, you want to please your boss and coworkers. Your desire to please makes you extremely vulnerable and susceptible to being taken advantage of and manipulated by these people. Your boss or coworkers may ask you to do things that are inappropriate, or you may do things *you think* you are supposed to do when in fact you are not! It's called sexual harassment. If you ever feel sexual pressure of any kind at work, quit *before* you make a mistake. Get a new job. Take extra care to protect yourself in the work environment.

What can you do to protect yourself in different environments?

- Be aware of your surroundings—who's out there and what's going on.
- Walk with confidence. The more confident you look, the stronger you appear.
- Don't let drugs or alcohol cloud your judgment.
- Be assertive; don't let anyone violate your space.
- Trust your instincts and your stomach. If you feel uncomfortable in your surroundings, leave.

- Lock your car door and windows, even if you leave your car for just a few minutes.
- Watch your keys. *Don't* lend them. Don't leave them. Don't lose them. And don't put your name and address on the key ring.
- Watch out for unwanted visitors. Know who's on the other side of the door before you open it.
- Be wary of isolated spots like underground garages, offices after business hours, and apartment building laundry rooms.
- Avoid walking or jogging alone, especially at night. Vary your route. Stay in well-traveled, well-lit areas.
- Have your key ready to use before you reach the door of your home, car, or work.
- Park in well-lit areas and lock the car, even if you'll only be gone a few minutes.
- Drive on well-traveled streets *with* doors and windows locked.
- Never hitchhike or pick up a hitchhiker.
- Keep your car in good shape with plenty of gas in the tank.
- In case of car trouble, call for help on your cellular phone. If you don't have a phone, put the hood up, lock the doors, and put a sign in the rear window that says, "Help. Call police."
- Always look in the back seat of your car *before* you get in to make sure no one is hiding there.
- *Immediately* lock your car doors after you get in. You don't want someone following you and getting into your car.

How can you help someone who has been sexually assaulted?

You can help someone who is abused or who has been assaulted by listening and offering comfort. Go with her or him to the police, the hospital, or to counseling. Reinforce the message that she or he is not at fault and that it is natural to feel angry and ashamed.[17]

Please look at Appendix B addressing what *immediate* steps to take if you or a friend has been sexually assaulted.

Chapter Thirty-nine ~

The Gray Area

Please don't stop reading this chapter—you *absolutely* need to know and understand everything I am about to say. Rape is a complex, sensitive, and horrifying subject. In the previous chapter, you read that rape occurs when you are "forced or *manipulated* into sexual contact, including vaginal or anal intercourse, oral sex, or penetration with a finger or an object, *without consent*." For purposes of this book, I limit my rape analysis to only two words in the above definition. The words are "manipulated" and "consent."

Each and every one of us is susceptible to manipulation. A goal of this book is to protect you from being manipulated. I want to keep you out of harm's way, to help you help yourself, to help you say *no* when necessary, and to help you avoid situations that can place you in danger. I want you to get up and leave when you know it's the right thing to do.

In Chapter 43, you will learn that if someone tells you a string of compliments including "You're special," especially in a sex-related situation, you are being manipulated. If someone purposely tells you all the things that you want to hear and want to believe are true, you are being manipulated. If someone has a goal in mind to take advantage of you and creates an environment where you do something that you never intended to do, and did not want to do, then you have been manipulated.

Some people can be manipulated with only a few words. It may take more time for others to fall victim to manipulation. The more determined someone is to manipulate you, the more likely he or she will succeed, if you are not cautious and aware.

Sometimes the manipulation is so subtle that you have absolutely no idea you are being set up. Date or acquaintance rape is a perfect example. You agree to go somewhere with someone who *seems* nice, and you're manipulated and do something you don't want to do. You must be very careful BEFORE you agree to go out with someone you don't know well enough to be alone with. You have to *anticipate* what might happen and decide how well you know him and how comfortable you are. Appearances can be deceiving.

The person accused of date or acquaintance rape will always claim that you "consented," and he will always say that you were not "manipulated." After all, you voluntarily spoke with him, met with him, went with him, kissed him, touched him, and allowed him to touch you. You never said "No," you never stopped at any point, and you never got up and walked away. You knew what was likely to happen *before* you went with him. He will say you got what you wanted or what you asked for. As far as he is concerned, you were not manipulated.

He will argue that you consented. But did you? You may have made a series of mistakes when you spoke, met, went, kissed, touched, didn't say *no*, and didn't stop what happened. You could have avoided the situation entirely by not going out with him. And, yes, you could have stopped or said "No" at any point along the way. You will have to understand and address these issues. But does this mean you were not manipulated? Maybe you just didn't know how to stop it. Maybe you didn't realize you could just get up and leave. You did not want what happened to happen. You did NOT consent! *Or did you?*

Has this happened to you? If so, did you *consent* or were you *manipulated?* That's the gray area. Will a jury of twelve of your peers agree with you?

Rape does not have to be physically violent.

Chapter Forty ~

Learn the Lesson, Grieve, Forgive Yourself, and Move Forward

*A*lthough I am writing this book to help protect you from making mistakes, we ALL make mistakes. We all have faults. No one is perfect. Often, we have to make mistakes to determine who we are NOT and to figure out who we are.

Sometimes you won't understand how good things are until you make a mistake and something bad happens. There are so many things and people we take for granted in life, including ourselves. Maybe it takes something bad to happen to begin to fully understand and appreciate what you actually have, and what you may have lost. The fear and pain associated with your mistake will open you up and awaken you to the treasures inside of and around you. That fear and pain will help you avoid the same mistake in the future.

Never let a mistake hold you hostage. Don't let a mistake distract you from who you are and who you want to be. Remember, one mistake does not define who you are. Don't let your past control your future. At the same time, keep in mind that if you make the same mistake again, you ARE well on your way to defining who you are. Think twice. There is an old saying: "Trick me once, shame on you; trick me twice, shame on me." If you make the same mistake more than once, you have no one to blame but yourself. Try hard *not* to let it happen again.

Always be cautious. Don't drop your guard. Avoid situations and people that put you in harm's way. Listen to and trust your stomach. Look for warning signs to protect yourself from repeating a mistake. If you make the same mistake a second time, you need to talk to someone you trust to understand why.

When you do make a mistake, LEARN THE LESSON, grieve, and forgive yourself. You made the mistake for a reason. It happened to teach you something important about who you are and *who you're not*. When you learn from your mistake and you realize that the mistake you made does not reflect the person you want to be, then you have grown and you are one step closer to figuring out who you are *not* and, in turn, who you truly are. **Let that mistake define who you are NOT!**

If what happened is weighing heavy on your mind and heart, please get it out—don't keep it bottled up inside. Talk to your parents and people you trust. Use the monologue in Chapter 24. The sooner you unload the burden, the sooner you will heal, grow, and move forward. Set yourself free.

You may *want* to forget what happened and avoid the painful memory. I understand how you feel, but I want you to consider another approach. *Think* about what happened. Remember it, and allow yourself to get upset, angry, feel frustrated, and then turn that pain and emotion into resolve, determination, commitment and certainty. Turn that negative experience into a positive by empowering yourself, focusing, and enabling yourself to stay strong the next time you feel uncertain or vulnerable. Remember the mistake well enough to never let it happen again. Ever! You can absolutely do these things to help yourself avoid the situation entirely the next time a similar situation presents itself.

I guarantee that similar situations will be presented to you again and again throughout your life. Alcohol, drugs, and every other vice will always be there and available. It doesn't stop. Even when you are an adult, sex can be tempting and you can be manipulated. It can be *anyone at anytime* and anyplace: your best friend's boyfriend, your boyfriend or husband's best friend, your brother-in-law, your boss, a coworker, anyone at work, the gym, or on girls night out! They can *all* be sources of temptation.

The facts and faces may change, but every day throughout your life you will be required to make decisions that affect you and the lives of the people around you. The truth is that you will always have to make the conscious effort to avoid people, places, situations, and vices that can hurt you and the people you love. It never ends. Never.

The good news is that when you learn from your mistakes, next time you will know better how to protect yourself from the start. Next time you will avoid the situation entirely. You will know how to respond at each and every step along your decision-making process. You will be more prepared, confident, capable, and able to handle yourself.

The lesson may be hard to learn, and it will take some time to get over the mistake you have made, but time heals all wounds. I promise you that you will grow stronger every day. Your potential is unlimited. Next time, you will have the opportunity to do the right thing and make the right choice. When you do, you will feel the warmth, confidence, strength, and inner peace of knowing that you protected and respected yourself and the people you love.

The Media Hype

Facebook, Email, Webcams   139

Sex and Porn in the Media and Internet   143

Chapter Forty-one ~

Facebook, Email, Webcams

Facebook is a great way to socialize with *friends that you know*. It's also a great way to ruin your reputation and life. It's your face on Facebook. What you show on Facebook, you show to the world. What people say on your wall, they say to the world about *you*. The photos you show on Facebook represent to the world who you are, where you've been, what you do, and with whom you socialize. Of course you can get a bad reputation *without* being on Facebook, but when used in the wrong way, Facebook can help you get that reputation faster. Inappropriate videos on YouTube are even worse. If you're not careful, Facebook and the Internet can be a huge problem.

Never put important and personal information on Facebook or the Internet including your address, cell number, home phone number, and social security number. Identity theft is a very real issue. Also be very careful what Evites or Facebook invites you send out. Would you announce on Facebook that you're having a party? Bad idea. I guarantee you that the wrong people will show up.

Also, you never know who is checking you out on Facebook or the Internet. Your parents, teachers, professors, college admission officers, and potential employers could be looking at you. Facebook stalking happens way too often. You just never know. And yes, Facebook entries often do have unintended consequences. I recently heard about a husband and wife who got divorced because of what was posted on Facebook!

Do you know all your friends on Facebook? If you have no idea who is asking to be your friend, don't agree. You've got enough friends, even if you have only one. You don't need friends you don't know. Consider it this way: Would you post your phone number and a picture of your face on a public bathroom wall so that unknown people could call you and ask to become your friend or maybe chat with you on the phone? I don't think so.

I read the newspaper this morning. A sixteen-year-old girl met a thirty-two-year-old man online using MySpace.com. She decided to come to California to meet her new "friend." He's now accused of forcing her into prostitution and threatening to send people to attack her family if she refused. He's been arrested and charged with coercing her into prostitution.[18]

Let me just say one thing about this incident. If someone *ever* threatens you or your family in any way, *immediately* tell your parents and call the police. Don't wait! NEVER ALLOW YOURSELF TO BE SCARED OR FORCED INTO DOING SOMETHING YOU DON'T WANT TO DO! NEVER!

Let's change the subject and talk about email, ichat and Webcams. Be very careful about what you write in emails, or show in YouTube videos or Webcams. Emails and Webcams provide only an *illusion* of privacy. Although you may think what you write in your emails is private, it's absolutely not!

The contents can be shown to the world. So can your iphoto, ichat, and Webcam videos and pictures.

I'm told that boys may ask you to expose yourself over the Internet. You may think that you're in the privacy of your home and nobody is watching. The problem is, you don't know who's on the other side of the Webcam. Even if the boy tells you no one else will see, the reality is you just don't know, and *he is trying to manipulate you.* In one case, I heard that the girl's naked photo is now the screen saver on the boy's computer. Please try to use your common sense.

Do you want to see yourself on YouTube or the Internet or be the screensaver joke of all the boys? How would you feel if you had to sit with your parents and explain certain pictures or videos of you? Be very careful about what you tell and show the world. It's your reputation. It's your life. Guard it. Defend it. Protect it.

One last point about cell phones and text messages. Never use either when you are driving. Not only is that illegal in some states, but you're putting yourself and others at risk. Also, don't forget common courtesy. Don't answer your phone every time it rings. If you are with other people, it may be rude to do so. You can often tell by the ring tone if you need to immediately answer the call. The same goes for text messages. Don't view and respond to them if you are in the middle of a conversation with someone else. Take a peek at your earliest opportunity but not right then and there. It's just common courtesy and respect.

I know it's almost impossible to live without the Internet. Just don't allow technology to blind your good sense and judgment.

Chapter Forty-two ∼

Sex and Porn in the Media and Internet

The media, Internet, and pop culture have tainted your environment. Much of what you see on TV, in movies, and on the Internet is garbage! You see celebrities acting like idiots. You see sexy styles and revealing clothes. You see music videos and hear song lyrics that portray girls as sluts. It's degrading.

What you don't realize is that the media is all about influence and money. Often media is used to sell sex, alcohol, drugs, and *more* sex to convince you to buy their products. You're making them rich when you buy into their hype. The media don't care if you got bad information or the wrong message. They want you to pay to watch their movies, wear their clothes and buy their products. The more you buy into what they're selling, the more money they make.

They don't give a damn about you! They don't care if you pay the personal price by buying what they sell. They don't care how you look in their clothes. They don't care about how you are perceived by the world. You are their personal billboard. You are not important to them, but your money is. Don't let the media and the Internet set your standards in life.

Watch out for subliminal seduction. Subliminal seduction means that the media are trying to influence who you are, what you do, and, most importantly to them, ensure that you spend your money on their products. TV commercials, magazine advertisements, and ad campaigns contain different forms of subliminal seduction and hidden messages intentionally designed to unconsciously hook you.

Look at the half-dressed models on billboards as you drive. What about the jean advertisements where three of the four buttons are unbuttoned. What do you think they are selling? Sex, sexy clothing, and pornography sell. The next time you look at an advertisement in a magazine, look hard to find hidden messages. Notice what the people in the ads are wearing or not wearing. Look closely at the location of objects in the ads, and you will see how their placement suggests sex. The messages are subtle but often present. Don't be manipulated and seduced by this garbage.

Let's look at another issue. If you ever see pornography, please never think that what you see is expected of YOU. You absolutely are NOT expected to do the things seen in the media. What you see is absolutely NOT what everyone does. *Never give your body away or allow it to be used or abused for someone else's pleasure because you think that's what you are supposed to do.* That's just wrong. You are NOT a toy to be used for someone's recreation.

I am so sorry to tell you that what you see in those pictures may not be what you think. The people in those photographs may not be willing participants. There is a terrible, terrible sex trade in this world where girls and women are kidnapped every day and are forced to do things you may see on the Internet. Many of those women are forcibly raped and abused. Don't let the Internet set your standard of conduct.

In addition, reality TV shows may be fun to watch, but they're not real. Ask yourself as you watch these shows, *Is this something I would do? Is that who I am or who I want to be?* Don't let the media and pop culture influence you to open the wrong doors. Avoid using actors and actresses as your role models in life. That's not who you are. Expect more from yourself.

You're smart. You know how to think. Never allow yourself to act like a machine. *You are a thinking, feeling, and sensitive human being.* Remember your family. *Remember where you came from.* Only you decide what you do and don't do. Don't let the media and Internet suck out your brain. It's hard enough being a teenage girl. It's even harder when so much of the media and Internet garbage surrounds, invades, and takes over every aspect of your daily life.

Finally, never let your friends, who buy into and *reinforce* the media hype, influence YOU to do the wrong thing. YOU are smarter than that.

Watch the media less and watch out for the media more.

Manipulative Boys

"You're Special"—That's Bullshit!   149
You Don't Owe Him Jack   153

Chapter Forty-three ~

"You're Special"—That's Bullshit!

Teenage girls are vulnerable and can be easily manipulated into doing things that they really don't want to do.

Girls want to be noticed, appreciated, and given attention. *Manipulative* boys who want something from you will *flood you* with compliments, "You're beautiful, you're not like the other girls, I love you. You're the one I want to be with. You're unique." Then you hear, "You're special." THAT'S PURE BULLSHIT! Although not all boys are like this, absolutely no boy of good caliber will overwhelm you with compliments and then tell you "You're special" unless he wants something. That something is SEX! Let's get blunt. He wants to get in your pants! Last night he told someone else the same line. Today he told you. Tomorrow he'll tell the next target.

I'm not talking about the boy that you've spent a lot of time with—someone you know well and trust. I'm talking about the player who's coming on to you much too fast.

Now is a good time for me to mention something. I have struggled with my use of the word "bullshit" in this book. How can I ask you to respect yourself when I am being so crude? This is how I see it: I know that what I'm saying sounds crude, but you *will* remember this harsh word at the right time. Fifteen years ago, I had the "You're Special"—That's Bullshit! conversation with a group of fifteen-year-old girls. Six years later, one of them thanked me. She told me she almost had sex with a boy who tried to manipulate her with the "You're special" line. He was coming on to her too fast. At first, she didn't realize what was happening and she was going along, but when she heard his string of compliments followed by "You're special," she *instinctively stopped*, told him he was full of shit, got up and left. She made my day. It is my hope that the word "bullshit" will resonate in your head, and *if necessary*, trigger a similar response.

Don't judge a book by its cover. Don't make the mistake and fall for the hot guy, the player, the bad boy, or the jerk. Don't be impressed or fooled by a "tool." You know a "tool" when you see and hear one. He looks good. He sounds good. But he's no good! He's a wannabe. He's a guy who is shallow, selfish, self-centered, and easily impressed by himself and by nonsense. He talks and brags because he has no depth. He's only interested in status, money, attention, and objects (YOU). He may be saying truthful things when he describes your beauty, but he's deceiving and misleading you as to his true intentions and motives. He is not genuine or sincere. He views you as a number and a notch on his belt. He's full of himself! Don't be his next victory or victim.

Often, it's a much older boy manipulating a younger girl by saying that she is special. Be cautious and watch yourself with older boys. But remember, it can be *any* boy. Whoever the boy is, he knows what he's saying and why he's saying it. He adds the "special" line to the end of his string of compliments to get him what he wants. SEX! *You will most likely hear this line immediately before doing something you don't want to do. Be aware. Think twice. Don't let it happen!*

There is another get-in-your-pants strategy going around. Manipulative boys will play the sympathy card. They will tell you about their hardships and how terrible things are going for them in their lives. They will lie through their teeth to make you feel sorry for them. They are playing on your sympathy and vulnerability. Don't fall for it. It's more bullshit!

If you ever hear a boy give you a string of compliments followed by "You're special," or "You're unique," remember that he is full of shit. Immediately tell him he's full of shit and leave the situation. If he gives you the sympathy line, don't buy into it. You're not his therapist.

If by chance you have never heard the special line or lie before, please don't be upset by what I'm saying. I understand how you feel when someone gives you a compliment. Even if you realize the boy's a player or he might be lying, you may not want to admit it. You may be so happy that *this time he is saying it to you,* that you may ignore your caution. Take the compliment, say "Thank you," but please *never* let the compliment blind you.

Also remember, if you say *no* and then a boy ignores you because you said *no,* don't fall for the silent treatment. Often, when a boy doesn't get what he wants from you, he gets mad and will ignore you. You then feel bad and may want to once again get his attention and to please him. Don't fall into that trap! So what if he's mad at you? Don't care if he ignores you. If you said *no*, you meant *no*. Never change your mind because he's manipulating you with the silent treatment. If he ignores you, he's doing you a favor. Remember, you said *no* for the right reasons. Stay strong. If you change your mind and say *yes*, he wins, and you lose.

One last point: If you fell for the special line, you're not alone. Keep reading. You won't let it happen again.

Chapter Forty-four ~

You Don't Owe Him Jack

Who's Jack? Jack is not a person. When I say, "You don't owe him Jack," I mean, you don't owe him *anything.*

You get compliments. You get gifts. He buys you a ring. He takes you out. He tells you you're beautiful. He says all the things you want to hear. What do you owe him? NOTHING. YOU DON'T OWE HIM JACK!

If he tells you you're beautiful, he's right. You don't owe him anything for telling you something you already know. That's right, you're beautiful!

If he tells you you're funny, he's right again!

He says to you, "You're not like the other girls." Well, duh!

If he gives you flowers, that's great. Take them. Say, "Thank you." You don't need to kiss him because he gave you flowers. Always remember: YOU DON'T OWE HIM JACK! You didn't ask for the flowers but, hey, it's great that you got them. They smell good. Put them in water when you get home. They look great on your desk. Enjoy them.

Never feel pressure to give something in return just because a boy says or does something nice. *You are being played!* Your body is not merchandise. You can't be bought. You don't have to kiss him. You don't owe him anything! If a guy expects something from you in return, he is absolutely the wrong guy for you. Let him take his expectations somewhere else. You don't want anything to do with him!

Finally, if he's stupid enough to tell you you're unique or special, don't even be nice. Just tell him he's full of shit and go home.

YOU DON'T OWE HIM JACK.

Relationships and Sex

What Will You Get by Giving a Blow Job
    or Having Anal Sex?   157
Why Are You Rushing to Have Sex?   163
Think Before the Morning After   169
Sex Is Often the Beginning of the End   171

Chapter Forty-five ～

What Will You Get by Giving a Blow Job or Having Anal Sex?

Your parents may be uncomfortable addressing this topic, but someone needs to speak out, so here goes. Blow jobs and anal sex are **not** safe sex! Blow jobs and anal sex are a big deal. There is absolutely nothing casual about oral or anal sex. BOTH ARE SEX!

What is your definition of safe sex? Does it simply mean that you won't get pregnant? That's much too simple of an analysis. Blow jobs and anal sex are not a form of contraception!

Does your definition of safe sex include herpes, gonorrhea, hepatitis B, syphilis, chlamydia, chancroid, HPV (visible or *invisible* genital warts known to cause cervical cancer), mycoplasma and ureaplasma infections, and even the possibility of being infected with HIV? All can be transmitted by oral and anal sex.

You know that STDs are sexually transmitted infections and diseases. STDs have different symptoms and often have no symptoms at all. STDs are so much more than a mere inconvenience. Different STDs have different serious health and risk complications. The consequences of an STD are far more serious for women than for men. If untreated, some STDs, including herpes, can impact your ability to get pregnant and to bear children. If not properly handled, herpes and other STDs can be passed on to your unborn children. This is particularly concerning because when herpes sores are active, herpes can be transmitted to another person, not only through sex but simply by kissing. Such a simple act can have lifelong consequences. *Even worse*, herpes can be transmitted when sores are *not* visible.

Imagine this: You get one of these diseases in high school or college. It's incurable. Are you prepared for the STD breakouts? Are you ready to take the steps *required* to stay well and to protect other people from getting the STD from YOU. How are you going to explain it to your future boyfriend or future husband? How will you describe what you did to get this disease? What will you say? How will he respond?

Don't think you can ignore these sexually transmitted diseases because you're young and in high school or college. Don't be so naïve. Remember the statistics in Chapter 36.

If it's already happened to you and you have, or have had, an STD, then take the very best care of yourself and the people around you. You're smarter and wiser now. You know better how to make good choices as you focus your attention, make your way through life, and accomplish your goals.

No matter how careful you are, *you are not immune!* I get so tired of *saying* and *seeing,* "Bad things happen to good people." But it's true. STDs are very real and the consequences can be devastating. Think this through—not only must you worry about where the guy has been, you can't ignore the history of each and every girl who got there before you. That's a lot of baggage for a one-time visit.

From a boy's perspective, blow jobs and anal sex are great. The boy gets pleasure while thinking there is no possibility of getting someone pregnant. If you're with the wrong boy, he adds a notch to his belt of girls who were naïve, curious, young, foolish, insecure, *and* WILLING to perform this act or simply didn't know how to say *no*, did not know how to stop, or just didn't get up and walk away.

From a girl's perspective, I understand you want attention and affection, and you may think that this is one way of getting it. The problem is that you're getting attention **not because of WHO you are, but rather because of WHAT you are willing to do.** This is absolutely not the kind of attention you want!

You may even be proud because you were able to satisfy the boy. Don't be so impressed with yourself—it doesn't take much to make him happy!

You may also think that you are *expected* to do this. You are so wrong! *Even if you've been in a long-term relationship, you should never, never give someone a blow job just because* **you or he *thinks* that's what you're supposed to do, or it's time.** NEVER! What does long-term mean to you? One week? One month? A few months? Let's get real—just how easy are you? Never assume that you are *expected* to do this. There is no such *expectation. And if there is, you are absolutely with the wrong guy!*

Don't allow yourself to fall into the trap of thinking that you will lose him if you don't have sex. Even though you're a couple, if all he wants from the relationship is sex, he's not interested in WHO you *really* are at all. The boy pressuring you with this kind of attention is absolutely not the boy you want in your life.

Don't allow yourself to be manipulated. Do what's right for you, on your own terms, at the time that's right for you.

Let me ask: Are YOU the girl who will get into a relationship in order to justify having sex? You may rationalize your decisions and think that it's OK to have sex because he's your boyfriend and you're in a relationship. You're wrong! He's wrong! Have more self-worth and self-respect. Do the math. How many boyfriends can, or did, you have in one year? Now finish the calculation. How many blow jobs can, or did, you give?

I really want you to think about this: Are YOU the one being the aggressor by suggesting, encouraging or offering to give a blow job or to have sex? If so, you must STOP! GET YOUR HEAD OUT OF THE CLOUDS AND GET YOUR FEET BACK ON THE GROUND. **OPEN YOUR EYES.** *Take a deep and serious look at yourself to determine who you are and exactly what you're doing and why.* WHY? **WHAT *EXACTLY* ARE YOU TRYING TO PROVE?** Very few boys will *really care, respect you, and say no* if you're so willing and offering to just give it away.

Ask yourself, *What will I, or did I, gain by giving a random blow job?* Will you get any benefit at all? I'll give you the answer. You will gain, or have gained, *absolutely nothing.* Let's break it down so it's easy to understand.

Will you respect yourself? No.

Did you act with dignity? No.

Will you respect your family or the people you love? No.

Will your family and the people you love respect you? No.

Will the boy have any respect for you? Absolutely not. He just used you.

Is that who you are or want to be? That's up to you.

Is this the reputation you want to have? That's up to you. Is that how you want to be remembered? That's up to you. The same goes for anal sex.

What concerns me is the general thinking nowadays that blow jobs are safe sex, are expected, are no big deal, and are acceptable conduct. *That's absolutely not true!* Blow jobs and anal sex are not safe sex. Blow jobs and anal sex are not funny, not casual and should never be taken lightly. Ignore the degrading music videos, song lyrics and media hype. Ignore your friends, their mistakes, and their bad decisions. Don't let the social attitudes of your generation change the morals and beliefs that you were raised with. Have higher expectations of yourself.

Ask yourself, and really think about your answers to, these questions: *How old am I? If I'm doing these things now, what comes next? What more will I do in the next one, two, and even three years? How old will I be then? What road am I going down? How many blow jobs do I have to give to wake up and understand that I am making a mistake and only hurting myself? How many is too many?* **Is that who I want to be? Is that how I want to be remembered?**

Girls, this is black and white. There is no gray area. Either you do it or you don't. Either you did it or you didn't. If you did it, it's because you made the choice to do it. **You may have made a mistake, but you didn't do it by mistake!** Don't fool yourself and think that blow jobs and anal sex are OK because you're saving your virginity for marriage. *That's nonsense.* What exactly are you saving if you've had almost every form of sex except intercourse? Get real! You're only fooling and disrespecting yourself. There is *absolutely* no way to rationalize your decision.

Blow jobs and anal sex are *not* lesser forms of sex. Blow jobs are equivalent to sexual intercourse. Anal sex is equivalent to sexual intercourse. They are on the same level. They are absolutely both sex.

One last thing: Have you ever heard of "friends with benefits?" That's a situation where you feel close enough to someone that you casually hook-up and maybe have sex, even though you are *not* a couple. The word benefit means you are *giving away* to your friend the liberty to have his way with you and your body. The problem is that YOU may be the only one *doing the giving*! You are allowing yourself to be used.

You are absolutely not in charge of your life and your body if all you're doing is pleasing him. Really think about this and ask yourself, **What benefit did I get?** If this paragraph applies to you, you may want to reread this chapter again, along with Chapter 18 about respecting yourself. Don't be so casual and careless with your body and your actions.

By the way, he can be the nicest guy in the world. That's really not important. This book is ALL about YOU, not him!

With all of my heart, I want you to understand that your body, your love, and your intimacy are all *gifts*. These gifts belong to YOU. They are *your most precious gifts in life*. Please don't give your gifts away randomly. Protect, honor, and cherish your gifts. Hold them close to your heart. Save them for the right time, the right place, and the right person.

Chapter Forty-six ~

Why Are You Rushing to Have Sex?

I asked Karen, a fourteen-year-old girl, "What's the hurry? Why are you rushing to have sex?" We talked for a while, and she shared her thoughts. Karen went to two different high schools. The first school had a lot of cliques, and the girls were very mean and promiscuous. The second was not that way at all, and she could just be herself.

Karen tried to explain that, at the first school, the other girls looked down on her because she was still a virgin. She felt that the more experienced girls thought of her "as still a baby." She thought the girls with more experience were cool and more popular. They had more boyfriends. They were liked more. They seemed to hold a higher level in the girl-community than the girls who were not sexually active. They were more mature and sexier than other girls. She said that all these things put pressure on her to "do more to put herself out there" in order to get to a higher status. It was her chance to be more like them.

I asked her if she really wanted to be like the other girls who put-out. She said there was a kind of "excitement and thrill" that she felt when she daydreamed about being on the edge and doing things she wasn't supposed to. At the same time, she explained that she really didn't want to do what they were doing. That wasn't who she was or wanted to be.

She felt the only way to be accepted was to be sexually active with a lot of boys. She said she was insecure. She thought that the only way to get attention and to be loved was to put-out.

Karen said, "It's so hard to be good when everyone around you is doing it or talking about doing it." She said she changed who she was to become more like the other girls because she wanted to fit in. She thought she wanted what they had.

She told me that the more she became like them, the more she lost and forgot who she was. The more she lost herself into their world, the unhappier she became. She never realized how much she changed and lost herself just to be like these other girls.

I asked her what she thought the boys thought of her. She told me that if she were a virgin, most guys would stay away from her because they knew they wouldn't "get with her." She added there would be a handful of guys who would go after her for just that reason. Each wanted to be the one to take her virginity. She thought the boys would think being a virgin meant she was a prude. I explained that not all boys think these things.

I asked her if it was the guy or the act of having sex that was most important to her. She wasn't sure. She said she hadn't yet met the right boy who she truly loved and wanted to have sex with. She said it must have been the act itself that seemed so urgent at the time.

I asked Karen, "Is the social status of having sex really that important to you? Is that the reputation you want to have? What happens if you get pregnant? Would you keep the baby? Would you want to have an abortion? How would you feel about these very real possibilities? How would you explain this to your family or future husband? What would you say? How would you feel about yourself? Is the *three* minutes of sex worth the sorrow and lifelong consequences? Are you ready for all of these things?"

The possibilities and questions seemed to overwhelm Karen. Although she knew these things were possible, she really hadn't thought them through. She thought that these things could never happen to *her. She thought she was immune.*

I could tell that she wanted to ignore these possibilities. She didn't want to face the reality, the details, and the consequences associated with pregnancy and abortion. I was deeply concerned for her, and for all of you, when I heard her answers.

I asked her to read the "Figure out Who You're Not" and the "Confidence and Self-Esteem" chapters. I wanted her to know everything in those chapters, so she could have the strength to be herself, to protect herself, and to slow herself down. I let her know that she absolutely did not have to be ashamed to be a virgin—*she should be proud, not embarrassed.* I told her, *"You absolutely don't have to rush to have sex."*

We sat together while she read. She liked the chapters and said that she appreciated the truth in them. She told me she wished she'd had this book earlier, and she was glad she had it now. She also explained that after she changed schools, she rediscovered herself. She liked herself a lot more in her new school. She could just be herself with all the other girls who were happy just being themselves. She was no longer suffocating herself. She no longer felt rushed to have sex. She was no longer lost.

After talking to Karen, I truly realized that there is only one first time in life. First kiss, first love, first whatever. You will never forget your firsts. They will be forever ingrained in your memory and will become a part of who you are.

I want you to take a minute to consider these thoughts and ask yourself these questions:

1. *Is this the boy I want to always remember as being the person I lost my virginity to?* It's a very important question. You will *never, never* forget this person, the time, the place and this event. How will it be remembered?

2. *Do I even want to remember this person at all? Do I want to always question what I did with this person and why?* You will *never* forget your bad choices. Don't let it happen if you don't want to remember it.

3. You've held off so far in high school. Now you're in college, and it's girls gone wild. You're living in the dorms. You've waited so long, and you're tired of being good. You're frustrated, so you give it away. What happens when you lose your virginity in the first few months of college? Are you ready for the emotional reality that you are no longer a virgin? You saved it for so long and now it's gone. You gave it away to whom? Where? When? Why? What good was that?

4. Do you think that having sex makes you more mature? If you think so, you're wrong! Do you want to have sex just to have sex and to get it over with, or because you actually love the person? There is a difference between infatuation and love. In reality, you can have sex almost anytime,

with almost anyone. All you have to do is smile, flirt, and offer to give it away. I've said it before—*very few boys will respect you* and pass up the opportunity to give you what you want.

5. Think about this for a minute. After your first time, what standard do you apply for when you will or won't have sex next? Are your standards lower or higher? What expectations do you have of yourself? Where do you go from there? Once again, that's all up to you and the choices you make.

6. There may come a day when you have a conversation with your own daughter about your first time. The story is more likely to be told if your *first* was a good experience. How do YOU want YOUR story to be told, if at all? Is this the person, time, and place you want to describe to your daughter, or is it better left unsaid?

7. If you've made a mistake with a boy, how will you feel each and every time you see him, even years later? Out of sight, out of mind? The reality is that even if you see him only once at your twenty-year high school reunion, or just by chance one night when you are out to dinner with your husband and family, you will instantly recall each and every emotion from twenty years earlier. I'm sorry, but that memory and pain never go away. And if your husband knows—he'll remember and feel it too. Since we are looking that far down the road, I want to mention one more thing. It may or may not be important to you or the guy you marry, if you even decide to get married, but some boys don't want to marry a girl who's been around or who has a reputation. You, too, may not want to marry the boy with that same reputation. It goes both ways.

Random sex is a bad idea. Rushing sex is also a bad idea. You will remember all your firsts. The more mindful and careful you are about who you're with, the less likely you are to have a painful memory. Be comfortable with who you are and where you are right now. Don't rush just to have sex. Slow down.

Chapter Forty-seven ~

Think Before the Morning After

The best way to fix a problem is to avoid it in the first place. You don't have to fix what's not broken. If you take the time to make a good decision in the first place, you will avoid having to worry about the multitude of consequences the morning after. However, if the morning comes and you need help, emergency contraception is available. *Don't wait.* Talk to your parents and people you trust. Be proactive and take the *immediate* steps necessary to get the help you need.

Chapter Forty-eight ~

Sex Is Often the Beginning of the End

You need to know that having sex is oftentimes the beginning of the end of a relationship. Before you have sex, there is something to look forward to in a relationship. After sex, there's often nothing left, so couples break up. Let's take a closer look at relationships and sex.

If you're not in a relationship and you start off with sex, that's more than likely where that "relationship" ends. Actually, there never was a relationship at all. Just random sex. To understand what happened, you might want to ask yourself these questions: *Why did I do that? What was I thinking? Was I motivated by the sex or the person? Is that who I want to be?*

If you're in a relationship that's going downhill, sex is not the answer to your problems. Break up and move on *before* you have sex. Don't make the common mistake of thinking that having sex will make everything better. You're absolutely wrong.

If you're in a relationship that's developing, introducing sex too soon may be the beginning of the end of that relationship. Rushing to have sex will only complicate, confuse, frustrate, and change the dynamics of that relationship. *Neither of you will know what is and is not expected of each other.* The rush for sex turns your relationship into an emotional riddle, a maze, and a roller coaster. That relationship will often lose its focus as the confusion surrounding whether or not to have intercourse overtakes the most important relationship requirement—true friendship. If true friendship is not present, there is absolutely no reason to be together.

If you're in that relationship and you do have intercourse, where do you go from there? What's left to look forward to? After sex, you often begin to realize that you really don't have much in common. The infatuation is gone, and you're really not sure why you're still with him. Sometimes you might wonder why you even started a relationship with him in the first place. You may keep the relationship going and keep having sex because you don't want to admit that you made a mistake.

Continuing the relationship justifies your original decision to have intercourse. That will carry you for a while, until you realize that intercourse alone does not make a relationship, and you *still* don't have much in common. If you're meant to be together, that's great, and the relationship continues. More often, you get bored, get tired of making *him* happy, and want out of the routine. Or, he gets tired of YOU. You break up and wonder why. You may ask yourself, *Was it worth it? Is that really* **who** *I wanted? Is that really* **what** *I wanted? Is that as good as it gets?* It's not. There's so much more.

The word "relationship" implies that you are able to actually relate on a number of levels with the other person. Ask yourself: *How well do you get along without being physical? How*

well are you able to talk with one another? How well do you under-
stand and empathize with each other? Is the person a close friend?
Is the person your best friend? How sensitive are you to the other
person's needs? Do you truly respect each other? Do you trust each
other? If so, how much? Are you honest with each other? Does he have
as much faith in you as you have in him? How much do you care
about each other? How much do you have in common? Is the other
person important enough to be someone you want in your life? Do
you know in your heart that you truly do love each other? Does this
person bring out the very best in you and make your life better? Do
you want to be with and date only this person? And finally, *Are all*
of these thoughts and feelings mutual?

All of these questions highlight just a handful of the ba-
sics for the existence of a real and lasting relationship.

When all these minimum relationship requirements
are met and sex enters the equation, a whole series of additional and more mature questions arise. The two of you
must comfortably be on the same page as to *each and every*
issue associated with having sex. You must fully agree on the
consequences of doing so. You must be actually prepared for,
and responsible to take, ALL of the precautions necessary to
protect each other and the people you love before you are
intimate.

If you are not able to fully address and comfortably agree
on all these issues, then you are not ready for sex. If you are
not able to fully commit to, and follow through, each and
every step required to have safe sex, then you are not ready
for sex. If either of you has any doubts at all, it's not the right
time. If you are disregarding yourself and YOUR expectations of yourself, it is not the right time. If it doesn't pass the
stomach test, it's not the right time. If what I am saying seems

way too complicated or overwhelming, then you are absolutely not ready to have sex. And most importantly, if you're *not* with the right boy, it's *never* the right time.

If you decide to have sex anyway, you're making that decision for the wrong reasons. Try not to allow curiosity, infatuation, peer pressure, frustration, or anger to be the foundation for your decision to have sex.

Never, never give your precious love away for the wrong reasons! Do everything in your power not to give your love away to the wrong people. Don't rush yourself. Forgive me for repeating myself—slow down. Allow yourself to just be a teenager.

I understand your natural desire to experiment and express yourself emotionally, affectionately, and sometimes sexually. These desires are inherent and powerful forces that are often difficult to control and can lead you into serious trouble. If you have sex with the wrong guy today, you're labeled and the talk of the town tomorrow. What do you do? How do you find the right guy—a *genuine and sincere boy of high caliber?*

This is how I see it. If you think you like someone or want to get to know someone, *never put yourself in the wrong place with him. Avoid a bad situation.* Make a point to meet him in a public place or somewhere you know *you cannot make a mistake.* Spend time and talk with him in this safe place. See if he's the kind of guy you like. Really listen to him. Learn what he's all about. Get to know him. Get together with him in this safe place on a number of occasions over a good period time—*several* months, not weeks. The longer the better.

Why so long? *Because you're giving yourself the opportunity to see his true colors and to see if you even like him. At the same time, you're giving HIM the opportunity to screw up before YOU make a mistake and screw up.* I've heard it said, "People are like leaves on a tree—they can change colors like the seasons." It takes a *full year* to see the colors change in all four seasons! Give yourself time.

You might discover you don't like him after all. You saved yourself the trouble of making a mistake. You don't hang out anymore. You might discover that he's getting tired of hanging out with you. That's not really what he's interested in. He doesn't want to *talk* at all. He's really not interested in YOU. *If all he wants is to get into your pants, he won't continue the charade.* He might decide that all of these visits are too much work just to get laid, so he'll stop hanging out and go after another girl who doesn't make him jump through the hoops.

You've got everything to gain and nothing to lose by getting together in a safe place. You avoid putting yourself in the wrong place at the wrong time with the wrong person. You're giving yourself time to evaluate and to avoid the pain and regret of rushing and making a mistake. You don't get labeled. And you don't become another notch on his belt and the talk of the town. You have no regrets!

Please remember that there is no set time for you to have any form of sex in your life. It's absolutely OK if it's not the right time, yet. There's a proper time and place for true love and intimacy. You will know in your mind, your heart, and your stomach when you are ready to open the door to intimacy. Listen to yourself. Trust and have faith in yourself. Don't minimize or take the decision to have sex lightly. Make these serious decisions when you are ready to be fully responsible for the consequences of your actions.

Remember, your gifts of love and intimacy are so very precious and beautiful. Please regard and protect your gifts with the high-

est degree of care and respect. Please never take yourself or your gifts for granted. Please respect yourself!

In my opinion, intimacy is the highest level of a relationship. It is so much more than sex. Intimacy is a private and personal matter between the couple and is not to be publicized. You will know who the right person is and when you have reached that level of intimacy. When you are with the right person, *together* you will know the right time.

I promise you that good things come to those who wait.

Consequences

Free Will   179

Alcohol is No Excuse for Bad Decisions   181

You Dodged a Bullet—This Time   185

Girls Have All the Power Over Boys   189

Wrong Place, Wrong Time   193

After Midnight   199

Don't Just Stand By and Watch—Do Something   201

How to Help a Friend in Need   205

Chapter Forty-nine ~

Free Will

Every one of us has free will. Free will means that you have the absolute ability to do anything you want. That's right. You have the free will to make any decision and choose what you do in your life. Your life is what you choose to make it.

You can get the best advice in the world, but whether or not you listen is totally up to you. Although you are free to make decisions, the consequences of your decisions are not free. They have been bought and paid for by the choices you make. Make the right choices. You have the power to decide. You have the power to say *no*. You have the power to avoid any situation within your control. You have more power than you realize.

Before you read this book, you had the excuse that you didn't know better, even if you knew deep inside that you actually *did* know better. Now that you've read it, that excuse is no longer available. Why? *Because now you actually do know better. You read the book!*

You know how to make good choices. You make good decisions every day. When you've exercised your free will and know you've made the right decision, *don't change your mind.* Your *determination and courage* will be tested. Stay strong. *You make your decisions by choice, not by accident.*

The people you love will be affected by the decisions you make. You will be remembered years later for your choices. Your life and the lives of the people around you will be changed by the decisions you make. Think twice, even three times, before making your decisions. Anticipate the outcomes of your choices, then choose wisely. Watch the good things that happen to you and the people around you when you make good choices. You will be pleasantly surprised.

Every day of your life you will have to choose between *what's right and what's easy.* More than likely, you will feel alone when you make some of your most important decisions in life. Your parents won't be there. People you trust won't be there. You will have to make the decision at that moment by yourself. Overcome your fear. *You have everything you need to make the right decision and pass this test.*

Try your best to always make a good choice. Use your self-control. Try your best to protect yourself and the people you love from your bad decisions. Try your best to always do the right thing. If you try, you can do it.

Free will is both a gift and a curse depending on how you use it. Use it wisely. You are the choices you make.

Chapter Fifty ~

Alcohol is No Excuse for Bad Decisions

Sorry, but using drugs or alcohol as an excuse for doing something wrong is nonsense, and you know it. *You weren't drunk before you decided to drink! You weren't high before you smoked that joint!* You can never blame *anyone else or anything* for YOUR decisions.

If you think it was OK to do x, y, or z because you were drunk or high, you're wrong! It's an excuse. You made the choice to drink or get high. You are responsible for that bad decision and for each and every consequence that flows from that decision. If you decide to make-out or even have sex and justify your actions because you were drinking, drunk, or high, you're full of it. Save the lame excuse. There is no excuse! *You did what you did because you wanted to.* Don't pretend you don't know it's true. It's that simple. YOU wanted to.

Don't go around blaming other people or things for YOUR thoughts and actions! Never blame the *victim* of your behavior for YOUR behavior.

If you decide to drive after drinking, you're putting your life and the lives of people around you in jeopardy. You're also exposing yourself to arrest and jail time for driving under the influence of alcohol. Never, never allow yourself or your friends to get into a car with a driver who's been drinking. NEVER!

When you see a friend or family member die or come close to death, you realize how fragile life is. Death is final. Do you want to live knowing that you killed a man, woman, or child because you chose to drive drunk? How will you feel for the rest of your life knowing that you're still here, but they're gone *because of you*? You don't want to be the driver in this news bulletin:

"A 16-year-old driver who was allegedly intoxicated when he slammed his SUV into a pregnant mother's car, killing her, her unborn baby boy and critically injuring her 6-year-old daughter, remains in police custody." [19]

This young family was in the wrong place at the wrong time, and now they're gone because he chose to drink and drive. Don't be that selfish.

The reality is that YOU DO KNOW BETTER. Whether you like it or not, YOU DO KNOW BETTER. Only you decide if you drink that beer or smoke that joint. Only you decide if you go to that party, get into that car, go to that person's house, or dress the way you dress. These are your decisions. You, and you alone, are responsible for your choices. If you make the better choice to avoid the situation entirely in the first place, you will never have a problem. You will have nothing to explain.

I understand that the more you drink the more difficult it is to make good decisions. I'm just reminding you that they are still *your* decisions. *Drugs and alcohol are not excuses for, and don't justify, your decisions and actions.* Your decisions start long *before* you go to that party.

Own your decisions.

Chapter Fifty-one ~

You Dodged a Bullet — This Time

We already know that everyone makes mistakes and that one mistake does not define who you are. Please keep one more thing in mind. If you make a mistake, you may be lucky enough to dodge a bullet *only once*. You may *not* get a second chance.

You may be painfully surprised to learn that YOU may pay a much greater price or have far more serious consequences than your friend who made the same mistake. Your one mistake can have lifelong consequences—drunk driving fatality, STD, pregnancy, abortion. You may have to drop out of school or college. You, and the people you love, will live with the public humiliation and private turmoil of your actions.

You may say, "This can't or won't happen to me." You're wrong!

Let me tell you about Stephanie. Shortly after turning fourteen, Stephanie had sex with her boyfriend and got pregnant in the summer *before* her freshman year in high school. She did not realize she was pregnant until the seventh month.

She did the right thing when she gave her daughter Alana to a loving couple for adoption. Alana has the most beautiful blue eyes I have ever seen. Stephanie is now a junior in high school and is taking honors and AP classes.

Let me tell you about sixteen-year-old Maria. She made the decision to attend her friend's twenty-first birthday party. She got so drunk that she passed out and found herself in a strange boy's car the next morning. To this day, Maria doesn't remember and has absolutely no idea what she did, he did, and what might have happened. Her older friends thought this was funny. Maria used to think like that; she no longer does. *She now wishes she could remember what happened.*

Then there was Sara. She graduated with honors from high school and was accepted to Princeton. She got pregnant in the summer before leaving for college. She decided to keep her baby. She never went to Princeton. Her life has been changed forever.

Shelly was a good girl from a good family and a freshman in college. We were close friends and classmates. She made the decision to have sex with a "hot boy" on the baseball team. She got pregnant and dropped out of school. I never saw her again.

Next was Sean. He was doing exceptionally well in college and had everything going for him. He broke his neck and died while diving into the shallow end of a swimming pool when he was drunk. Swimming pools, hot tubs, and alcohol are a dangerous and deadly combination.

Finally, there was a guy who drowned in his bathtub because he was drunk. By the way, he was an adult.

I don't know why, but people who regularly do bad things seem to get away with it, at least for a while. On the other hand, it's the good people who seem to have the problems and serious consequences resulting from their one-time bad decisions. That good person could be you.

YOU are the person who is more likely to have the problem because YOU are the least prepared.

If I am scaring you, that's good because I am scared for you. These are all very real things that you should be aware and scared of. Your friends may have had multiple chances, but you may not get a second chance.

Don't ignore and don't underestimate the potential consequences of your actions. Although YOU are not defined by a single mistake, don't ignore the reality that a single mistake can drastically change your entire life.

By the way, I recently heard that Sara and her little one are doing well. She's made the very most of the cards that life dealt her, and she is moving forward and working hard toward her goals.

I just need YOU to know that *not every story has a happy ending.*

Chapter Fifty-two ~

Girls Have All the Power Over Boys

Girls, you have ALL the power over boys. That's right. You have ALL the power over what you do, when, with whom, where, and how you do IT.

IT is everything **you** make the decision to do in your life. Everything! Absolutely no one else controls these decisions. Just you. Absolutely nothing within your control can or will happen without you making a decision. Nothing!

Please be very careful. Never use your power over boys as a weapon. Absolutely never, and I mean *never*, be overly aggressive or manipulative with a boy. Some parents refer to these as "predator girls." The boys often refer to these girls using the labels I described earlier. If you *are* manipulative, it will catch up to you much sooner than you think. I guarantee that when it does, you will NOT be happy!

Power can be used as either a sword or a shield. You must be cautious how you use it.

When used as a sword, your power over boys can get you into serious trouble and can truly ruin your reputation. Don't be so flirtatious that you're labeled a tease. That is absolutely NOT a good reputation to have. Boys don't like and have absolutely no respect for girls who tease. There is an old saying that describes a boy's perspective of a tease: Either put up or shut up. Being a tease is absolutely not the way to get a boy to like you. In fact, boys will avoid you and disregard you entirely once you earn the "tease" label. Your reputation will go down the drain. You will lose your power.

By the way, if you find yourself in a bad situation and you hear, "Put-up or shut-up," ignore it. Make the good decision to say *no* and get up and leave. It doesn't matter what someone says or calls you when you make a good decision to avoid a mistake.

What concerns me about using your power as a sword is when you are being an intentional tease in a sexual way with absolutely no intention of following through after being flirtatious. Don't do that. It's a lie, and people don't like or respect liars. As I said earlier, it will come back to bite you.

When used as a shield, you have the power to anticipate and protect yourself from the start. Use your power to be cautious, thoughtful, and to avoid bad situations. You'll have better control over your choices and your actions. You will avoid certain boys and situations when you know they can present a problem. You will know that it's a bad idea, and you won't go to the party in the first place. If you go, you will know to leave long before the trouble starts. You will better protect yourself from manipulation. You will understand that only you decide whether or not you're going to makeout, have sex, drink alcohol, or do drugs. You can use your power to protect yourself.

When you use your power as a shield, you are more able to enjoy life to the fullest, on YOUR terms, without putting yourself at risk. You will be much happier. You will have far fewer regrets.

You have ALL the power! Use it wisely.

Chapter Fifty-three ～

Wrong Place, Wrong Time

O K, girls, this is a really long chapter. Please hang in there with me because this rule is huge: *Take every precaution to avoid being in the wrong place at the wrong time.*

You have absolutely no idea how much trouble you can get into without ever doing anything wrong. All you have to do is be in the wrong place at the wrong time.

Let's start with an easy example. You're at a party. Pictures are taken. Things are happening in the pictures that shouldn't be. You are doing absolutely nothing wrong, but you happen to be in the pictures. The pictures get posted on Facebook, MySpace, or the equivalent. Those pictures are seen by the wrong people. Even though you're not doing anything wrong, you are guilty by association. You were in the wrong place at the wrong time.

Here are a few party rules to keep in mind:

- Anticipate what will happen at a particular place or party you are thinking of going to. If your stomach tells you it's a bad idea, don't go. Trust yourself. Trust your stomach.

- If you don't drive, learn to drive. One of the best ways to protect yourself is to drive to the parties you attend. You won't drink when you drive because that's not an option. When you drive, you can leave as soon as you want because you don't have to rely on someone else or wait around when you're ready to go.
- Drive by the party before getting out of the car. If you don't like what you see, don't go in.
- If you ignore your concern and still decide to go to the party, get there early before everyone is wasted—the end of the party is always the worst part.
- When you're at the party, if your stomach warns you that trouble is on its way, *get up and leave* long before the trouble starts. Otherwise, you could be in the wrong place at the wrong time.
- And finally, always stay out of the questionable pictures.

Let's take another more complicated example. Let's say you're at a party that's *not* at your house. The police bust the party. If you're lucky, they'll just warn you and leave. You go home. This time you dodged a bullet.

If you're not so lucky, you can end up sitting in the police station waiting to get picked up by your parents or another adult. Even though you should, you don't worry too much about this. You have absolutely no idea how close you are to what's next.

What's next? If you're really NOT lucky, you may spend the night in a holding cell with people you would rather not be with; trust me, this is not fun. You have now entered the real world and the legal system. That is *absolutely not* where you want to be. More about that later.

Last example: Your parents are gone for the night or week-end. Time to have a party? Sounds like fun to you? Sounds like a disaster waiting to happen to me.

The party starts off great. Just a few friends at your family home. You think you invited the right people, so everything will go smoothly. What if you're wrong? What if the people you invited get out of hand? What happens when the doorbell rings and uninvited people decide to show up? You may or may not let them in. If you *don't* let them in, who knows what they'll do. If you *do* let them in, who knows what they will do. This party was supposed to be fun. Now you're starting to wonder.

Will the boys, or even the girls, decide to fight inside or outside your house? Will your house get trashed? Will things get stolen? Will someone get injured on your parents' property? Will someone have sex in your parents' house and later claim they were raped? Will someone leave the house in a drunken state and then injure or kill himself, herself or someone else on the way home? Will your parents get sued because of these things that YOU let happen in *their* home?

You made the poor decision to have a party at the wrong place—your family home. You have now opened up a Pandora's box (a can of worms, a box full of unanticipated and irreversible consequences).

The financial and legal consequences to your family are endless. Your parents can be sued for what occurred in their home while they were away. Your parents have sacrificed, working long and hard to provide you with the home and life that you have. You have now put your parents' future and the financial security of your entire family in serious jeopardy. You finally made it! Welcome to the real world and the legal system.

Your parents do get sued. They hire an attorney with a $5,000 up-front deposit and an hourly rate of $250. That's cheap, by the way. Your parents take four hours to explain your side of the story to your attorney. That costs $1,000 and that's just the first of many meetings. Litigation may take one or two years thanks to interrogatories, depositions, and pre-trial motions. There will be lots of meetings, lots of hours. That's $250 for each hour of attorney time. There may be a trial at the end of the litigation. Trials could take eight hours a day. At $250 or more an hour, your parents just paid $2,000 for that *one day* of trial. Trials can take time—from one day to one week, one month, or even longer. Add it up.

By the way, while all these legal fees were being incurred, your parents were kept away from work and were not able to make the money necessary to keep the household going. This can financially ruin what your parents took years to build.

Let's put the financial devastation to the side. If what happened is really serious, it may end up in the newspapers. You, your family, and their good reputation are now in the headlines. The private and public humiliation is unrelenting. This can destroy the personal lives of your family members and your family name.

During this same time period, YOUR life and plans are also put on hold because you have no idea what's going to happen to yourself, your family, and your future.

This is not what you intended. All you wanted to do was have fun. You were just being a teenager. All you did was throw a party in your parents' home—a home you have the privilege, *not the right*, to live in.

I am not trying to scare you. This scenario is all too real. I spent years as a trial attorney protecting my clients from the risks and uncertainties of our judicial system. The legal system is absolutely one place you *don't* want to be. You are risking not only your parents' financial security, but even worse, you are actually losing control over your and your parents' lives by putting and placing your personal freedom into the hands of a judge or a jury of twelve people who have absolute control over your destinies.

Judges and juries are unpredictable. If a civil case is filed, your family's money is at stake. If a criminal case is filed, your personal freedom is at risk with the possibility of jail time.

By the way, you may think that if you are under eighteen, you have more leeway and the law will not be as harsh. Sorry, the rules have changed. Laws are being passed every day holding minors more accountable and to the same standard as adults.

You may think I'm going overboard, and none of this could ever happen to you. I hope and pray that you are right. But you're not! Always be open to the possibility that you may be wrong.

One last point: If your parents allow your friends to drink in their house, they probably have no idea what a mess they can get into. The fact that your parents knowingly allow this to happen exposes them to severe consequences. Many communities around the country are imposing new or tougher Social Host laws that make parents legally responsible if underage guests drink in their homes.

"Elisa Kelly thought she was doing the right thing when she bought $340 worth of beer and liquor for her 16-year-old son and more than 20 of his friends. In exchange for the booze, Kelly's son agreed that all his pals would sleep over at his birthday party. That, in the mind of the 42-year-old mother of two, was the best way to keep the underage revelers from drinking and driving. None of the kids who came to her home got hurt, but someone is indeed paying the price. Kelly went to jail this week to serve a 27-month sentence for providing alcohol to minors."[20]

If this is happening in your home, you may want to let your parents read this chapter for their own protection and the protection of your family. This is one of the situations where they need YOUR help.

One more last point: If you're foolish enough to throw a party in your family home and things get out of hand, call the police. Never ask people to leave, and never have a friend ask them to leave. This will often lead to fights and damage to your parents' home and possessions. Let the police clear out your house so you don't have to.

Make a point to be with the right people, in the right places, at the right times. Avoid the wrong people, the wrong places, the wrong times, and the wrong outcomes.

Chapter Fifty-four ~

After Midnight

*L*et's make this one short and simple. This is the rule:
When you're a teenager, *nothing good happens after midnight.*

Absolutely nothing!

Get off the street and get off the road.

Go home.

Chapter Fifty-five ~

Don't Just Stand By and Watch — Do Something

*K*now the difference between action and inaction. Action can be defined as doing something in order to achieve a purpose. Action requires some form of movement or energetic activity. Inaction is the opposite. Inaction can be defined as failing to take action when action is necessary. The definition implies sitting or standing idly by.

Let's look at some basic examples:

You know that something wrong or bad is going to happen, and you take no action to stop it from happening. Are you responsible for your failure to act?

You're at a party, and you just stand there and watch as the house is getting trashed. Are you responsible in any way for your inaction?

You're with a friend who decides to steal something. You say and do nothing. Are you responsible for your failure to stop this from happening?

Someone you know is doing things to hurt themselves or is threatening to hurt someone else. You say and do nothing. Are you responsible in any way for your failure to help?

You have information that you know will better a situation. Should you disclose that information or remain silent? Are you responsible if you disclose only part of what you know and omit crucial facts?

I am of the opinion that your failure to act in these situations is often caused by your simply not knowing what to do. You don't know how to help or if you will get into trouble for trying to help. If the issue is whether or not to help a friend, you may begin to question your own loyalty. You don't want to betray a friend. What do you do?

These are very serious, confusing, and overwhelming questions, especially if things are happening way too fast and these questions all occur to you simultaneously. Sometimes it feels easier to do nothing, but intuitively you know it's just not right. What do you do?

Here's the rule: *Don't just stand by and watch. Always do something. Anything.* Here are some tips:

1. Never feel that you are being disloyal by getting help for a friend who has asked you to keep a secret. If you know in your mind, your heart, and most importantly in your stomach that something bad is going to happen to someone you care about, take action to help. Call a parent, a teacher, or a counselor. Anyone and everyone you think will make the situation better. That's what real friends do. You would want them to do the same for you.

2. For minor issues, tell the person if you disagree with what he or she is about to do. Speak up. If he or she doesn't

listen and/or hassles you in any way, get away from the situation as soon as possible. You absolutely don't want to have anything to do with what is about to happen. You don't want to be *guilty by association*. Leave while you can. Don't be in the wrong place at the wrong time. If help is required, call for help.

3. For more serious situations where someone's health, life, or property can be harmed, *don't put yourself in danger in any way*. If there is no immediate danger, do your best to find help for the person in need. If the situation is urgent, immediately call someone you trust for help. Call anonymously, if necessary. Don't wait. Always seek out help if you know it's the right thing to do.

You never want to live with the consequences of your inaction, knowing that it was within your ability to make things right.

I recently read about three girls at a college party who rescued a seventeen-year-old girl who was drunk and being sexually assaulted. As the three girls were leaving the party that night, another female partygoer told them there was "a girl in a room with eight guys."

The three girls didn't think that sounded right. They had no idea who she was, but they went back upstairs to the party and knocked on the door. When the door opened, they saw the victim on a mattress on the floor being sexually assaulted. They shoved their way through the door and confronted the boys. One of the rescuers said, "The victim was so intoxicated she appeared to be comatose and that eight or more men stood around watching one of them sexually assault her." [21]

The rescuers got the guy off the girl and tried to get her on her feet. She was unable to stand. They asked the boys watching to help them carry the victim to safety. The rescuers were waiting for someone to step up, to be a man; instead, the boys drifted away like cowards. They carried her by themselves, took her to the hospital, and notified authorities.

There were boys in that room who could have stopped this situation and could have assisted the rescuers, but they *failed to act.*

I don't know and don't really care if the boys were on the baseball team, the lacrosse team, or whatever. I'm not impressed by them or their behavior. In my opinion, the boys are all cowards, all guilty by association, all equally responsible, all equally to blame, and all accountable for their actions as well as their failure to act when action was absolutely necessary. They will all have to deal with the moral and legal consequences of their actions and their failure to act.

Sadly, the rescuers later got hassled for doing the right thing. That didn't stop them from volunteering to testify in any court proceedings against the boys. I think the rescuers are awesome.

Don't just stand by and watch. Do something. Anything.

Chapter Fifty-six ~

How to Help a Friend in Need

You hear rumors that Jane is cutting herself. You're told that Sandy has an eating disorder. You see Jasmine with bruises on her arm, and you just know that someone is hitting her. You see Lisa drinking way too much, too often. Ann talks about killing herself. What do you do to help?

Just like the last chapter, don't sit and do nothing. Do something! Do everything you can to get help. You're NOT a doctor. You're NOT a counselor. Don't try to take care of this by yourself. You are NOT doing anyone a favor by delaying getting the proper help. You are absolutely NOT being a true friend by keeping this a secret. Call parents, teachers, and counselors. Keep calling and don't stop until you know that something is being done to help your friend in need.

Girls, this is not a game. If you see or hear things that you know are wrong, you may be able to better that situation. *All of you girls have an unspoken obligation to help each other.* One very simple way to help yourself is to help others. Take action.

You are not betraying or "ratting out" your friend when you seek help. You are saving a life. You are being a true friend.

In Appendix C, I have listed signs that may signal eating disorders, alcohol abuse, abusive relationships, and suicide. Now is a good time to take a minute to check out Appendix D which was written by a beautiful teen who wanted to contribute her thoughts to this chapter.

Hang In There and Go For It

Opportunities   209

The Graduating Boyfriend   211

Love   215

Adjust   219

This Book Is a Downer and Is Killing My Social Life   221

You Have a Blank Page   223

Allow Yourself to Be a Teenager   225

Chapter Fifty-seven ~

Opportunities

You just got cut from the team or the school play that you tried out for—something you really wanted. You're upset. You tried your best but things just didn't work out. What do you do now? I know it hurts, but don't let that setback stop you in any way.

There's an old saying: "When God closes a door, He opens a window." A window of opportunity.

Open your eyes. Look for the window. Every day the world will present new opportunities for you to consider. Your job is to watch for, and be receptive to, those opportunities. Select the opportunities that are best for you.

If you open yourself up to the right opportunities, you will be pleasantly surprised to find interests that have been waiting for your arrival. When you open the door and embrace a good opportunity, you will meet new people, make new friends, and discover new gifts and talents hidden inside you. Don't shy away from or deny your gifts or talents.

Keep in mind that *you have to act* when a good opportunity

comes your way. People who accomplish things rarely sit back and watch things happen. *Make positive things happen in your life.* Don't wait to be asked to join student council, the orchestra, or the clubs at school or elsewhere in your community. Volunteer and help out wherever you feel most comfortable and appreciated. Make it happen. Go for it. Enjoy yourself. Focus on the things you do well. Do what makes you happy. Try not to stress or get distracted by setbacks or by what anyone else thinks.

My father used to tell me, "You have eyes, you can see. You have ears, you can hear. You have a mouth, you can speak."

Use what you have. Give yourself the chance to try new things. Keep yourself busy. Be open to all that life has to offer.

Make the most of the good opportunities that come your way. Go for it!

Chapter Fifty-eight ~

The Graduating Boyfriend

This is a difficult subject. On one hand, if you're in a relationship that you don't know how to get out of, graduation is a great excuse to break up. On the other, if you actually love the boy, then there is no one way to answer exactly how to deal with the multitude of feelings and emotions associated with the graduating boyfriend. Your feelings and emotions are all very real. It may not be puppy love. You may have actually found your one, true love. He may be the boy you marry, or the one who got away. Either way, the emptiness that follows separation from or the loss of your first real love is often painful and deep.

How do you deal with this separation and loss? I have a few thoughts I hope will help or at least provide a bit of clarity in what can be a very difficult and emotional time.

If you are both in the same graduating class, realize that the two of you are just moving forward. Keep in mind that although you are a couple, you are still individuals. Don't make the mistake of going to the same college if that college is not the right match for you. Give each other the opportunity to grow as individuals. It's only then that you can truly grow together.

If you are not in the same graduating class, what I've said still applies with one added element. You are NOT left stranded behind; rather, it's now your turn to make the most of your remaining high school or college year(s), and his turn to do the same in college and thereafter. Do just that. Keep yourself busy. Enjoy yourself. Time will go fast. Always do your very best. Be as good as you can be. Leave your school being a better person and knowing that your contribution made it a better place. Soon enough, you will be graduating. Graduate feeling good about yourself and how you will be remembered.

Look forward to both the new opportunities you will have and the new people you will meet. That's exactly what will happen every day of your lives anyway, long after high school and college. Don't be scared or insecure about those opportunities and people. Believe in yourself. You will make good choices. Trust yourself and each other.

Some people say, "Absence makes the heart grow fonder."

Others say, "Absence makes the heart go wander." Exactly what will happen in the future will never be known. One of my favorite poets, Kahlil Gibran, says it beautifully:

"If you love somebody, let them go, for if they return, they were always yours. And if they don't, they never were." [22]

He also writes "… let there be spaces in your togetherness." [23]

Remember, life is full of hellos and good-byes. Both can pull at your heart and make you simultaneously happy and sad. I believe that some of the best times in your life will be those hellos and goodbyes and the anticipation in between.

I know that uncertainty creates stress and anxiety. It's OK to be afraid. That's where faith comes in. Keep the faith.

In my opinion, being the best of friends is as good as it gets in this situation. You really can't ask for a whole lot more because that's simply not realistic. Keep in touch. Say how you feel. Trust me, things always work out. And, if you're meant to be together, you will be.

Chapter Fifty-nine ~

Love

Love is not a game. There is no ball. There is no court. The foundation of love requires mutual trust, honesty, and respect. Love is so much more than a word. Relationships are never perfect, but the possibilities and depth of love are endless.

True and lasting love takes time, effort, and vigilance for two people working together to blend and share their gifts and talents. Each helps the other to overcome their weaknesses and pursue their strengths. Each is equal. Each has a say. Each receives the other's compassion, understanding, and empathy. Each takes the very best care of and "spoils" the other. Each makes a point to never, ever take the other for granted. Neither is blinded by pride. Neither misses an opportunity to right a wrong. Neither is selfish or self-centered.

They avoid the mistake of being complacent. They show their appreciation. They don't assume that one knows what the other is thinking and feeling. They work together to overcome disappointment, hardship and obstacles. They understand and accept that their thoughts, feelings, and opinions may not be the same on every issue. They understand and appreciate the difference between being caring and protective versus being controlling and overbearing. They consciously avoid people, places, situations, and temptations that can cause the other pain, uncertainty, embarrassment, anxiety, insult or humiliation. They make each other feel secure.

They understand that they are two different people with different needs. They are willing to confront and resolve their differences. They communicate with each other. They listen. They understand. They are open and willing to adjust and grow together. They are true to themselves and to each other. They understand the difference between needing their own personal space, which is healthy, versus being secretive which is a lie and is destructive. They understand the need to tend to, care for, and nurture themselves as a couple, in addition to caring for each other as individuals. They respect themselves and each other.

The person you love is your sanctuary, and you are theirs. That person keeps you safe, calm, and centered when the whole world seems to be falling down around you. That person makes you complete. There is a deep and hollow emptiness inside of you when you're apart or when you disagree with each other. You care for each other so much that sometimes your love can make you afraid. This is the person with whom you can't seem to stay angry. Things don't always have to be perfect, but most of the time they are, as long as you are together. That's why you love the person. You have all of these feelings not because you *think* you're supposed to, but because that's how you actually feel.

Love

What is love? The Bible says it best for me:

Love is patient
Love is kind
It does not envy
It does not boast
It is not proud.
It is not rude
It is not self-seeking
It is not easily angered
It keeps no record of wrongs.
Love does not delight in evil
but rejoices with the truth.
It always protects
Always trusts
Always hopes
Always perseveres.
Love never fails.

Chapter Sixty ～

Adjust

Do you want to know how to make God laugh? Tell Him your plans.

Things happen in life that you can't stop. You have to be prepared for change and be ready to adjust to whatever comes your way. Change is often not easy. If it's for the better, change is easy to accept. If it involves a loss such as illness, divorce, or death, change is often much more difficult. No matter what the change is, you must learn how to adjust.

If you have the ability to alter a negative change, then exercise your power. Never accept that which you have the ability to better. If the change is beyond your control, learn to accept and adjust to the new circumstances to the best of your ability.

Remember, the world turns every day. One day you can be on the top of the world, and the next day you can be on the bottom.

Never take anyone or anything for granted. *You may not have the person with you tomorrow.* Say "I love you" every day to the people you love; you may not have that chance tomorrow. We often forget that we are only given so much time. *The only gift greater than love is time.* Understand that every day of your life will bring both good and bad things that will happen to you, the people you love, and the world around you. Make the most of your time.

Always have faith. Never lose hope. Hope is a wishful prayer. Pray.

Be thankful for all that's good. Say "Thank you" throughout every day. Be thoughtful and gracious when things don't go your way. Adjust when there are changes in between. Life is like a merry-go-round—it goes up, and it goes down.

Hold on tight.

Chapter Sixty-one ～

This Book Is a Downer and Is Killing My Social Life

I'm not trying to ruin your social life by writing this book. It's your *life*, not your *social life* that I am interested in.

If I didn't think you were worth it, I wouldn't take my time writing this book. You may think I don't know you. You're right, but I know who you can be. I know what you are capable of. I have spent the last twenty-eight years talking to teenagers and young adults just like you. You all share so many beautiful things in common. What I discuss in this book relates to *all* of you. You are not alone. You are absolutely worth my time in writing this book.

I want you to have fun, go to parties, meet boys and girls, dance, laugh, sing, and have a great time. At the same time, I want you to always anticipate and avoid potentially harmful people, places, situations, and the type of *fun* that can blur your reputation. I want you to always be smart and safe. I want you to try your best never to cross the line. I want you to make perfectly clear to the world exactly where *your* line is so that there is *never a shadow of doubt about who you are, what you do, and where you stand*—by doing so, **I want you to define yourself!**

I want you to be confident, elegant, and hold yourself to the highest standard, a standard that is beyond compare. A standard that YOU can and will always be proud of. I am asking you to be your very best *all of the time.* When you walk into a room, I want everyone there to have the absolute greatest respect for you and to hold you in the highest regard**. I want you to always respect yourself.**

But far more important than what *I want* is what ***YOU want. YOU have to want all of these things. I am absolutely not asking any more of you than you should ask of yourself. Do these things for YOU—not for me—not for anyone else—only YOU!***

Don't worry, your life and social life will be great. Just keep on reading. We're almost finished!

Chapter Sixty-two ～

You Have a Blank Page

Fill it up! Keep trying. Always do your very best at everything you do. Make your dreams come true. Keep yourself busy. Take the steps necessary to change your circumstances and better your life and your world. Don't allow anyone to stand in the way of your dreams. You are unstoppable.

Always be on the alert when someone gives an opinion about YOU. Never let anyone's negative opinion of you, your abilities, or your good or bad choices limit the possibilities, hopes, and dreams in your life. Never limit your possibilities because someone else doesn't believe in you or in what you hope to accomplish.

One of my favorite quotes reads as follows: "The person who says it cannot be done should not interrupt the person doing it."

Let them talk—do your thing! There is only one way to guarantee failure in your life...to NOT try!

There's another old saying: "If you don't like the news, go

out and make some of your own." Go make good things happen in your life. Go make some news. I know you can do it.

That doesn't mean life will always be easy. And it doesn't mean that you will accomplish your every goal. But try. Keep trying. Then try again. Be persistent. Be resilient. When things get hard and don't go your way, take a break, rejuvenate, then go out there and work hard to finish what you started.

Take small bites. If you bite off more than you can chew, you may choke.

Your life is what you make of it. Do good things. *Show the world what you've got!* Write your own story.

Chapter Sixty-three ~

Allow Yourself to Be a Teenager

There's plenty of fun, parties, and good times to be had. It's all out there waiting for you.

Keep busy and make good things happen. At the same time, always remember there is no rush to do anything that you are not ready for. There is a difference between making things happen and rushing yourself. If you find yourself rushing, ask yourself, *What am I rushing for?*

When you rush, whatever you're doing ends quickly. Why end it now? It's more fun to stay in the game. You're only young once. Slow down. Save something for later.

Don't try to grow up so fast. There's plenty of time for that. Have fun. Do things that make you happy. Be yourself. You are beautiful and smart, and you need to remind yourself of that every day. Have faith in yourself. I promise that you will trust yourself more with each passing day.

Yes, there are times when you don't feel confident; you're confused and you feel insecure and unsure about yourself. That's perfectly OK. That's normal. When that happens, take a step back. Take a break. Take some time to find yourself. Withdraw. Cry. Talk, and keep talking to people you love and trust. Cry again, write, and keep writing—get it ALL out.

Give yourself time to get your courage and strength up and running again. Don't doubt yourself. When you doubt yourself, you doubt your courage. If you look deep inside yourself, you will find the strength and courage to get through anything and everything.

Be patient. Keep your common sense. Hold on to being a teenager for as long as you can. Have fun knowing that you have not tried everything and you still have so much more to discover in life. Allow yourself to be young. You're only young once.

Closing Thoughts ～

I love music. One of my favorite musicians, James Taylor, wrote some of my favorite lyrics. He wrote that "the secret of life is enjoying the passage of time." Enjoy the passage of time. Life is a beautiful journey. Enjoy the ride. Make it a beautiful ride. Just be thoughtful and careful.

Read the children's book *A House for Hermit Crab* by Eric Carle. It teaches you that the possibilities in life are endless. It also teaches that it is perfectly OK to shed and change who you are (your shell) when you need to move on and when you have grown. It's totally appropriate to make adjustments along the way.

Go to iTunes and download the song "Take Some Time" written by my son Andrew Dudum when he was a senior in high school. The song summarizes everything I'm trying to tell you. *Take some time to remind yourself. Close your eyes and breathe. Figure out who you are inside and where you want to be.* The lyrics in their entirety are in Appendix E.

I hope I haven't made you too tired by reading this book of my opinions, thoughts, rules, and "antidotes." I truly believe that this book will help you enjoy being a teenager and a young woman. I know in my head and my heart that it will help you to be stronger and safer in high school, college, and thereafter. I am certain your life will be so much better if you just consider what I am saying and apply what you have learned.

It's nice to have a guide of handy rules and strategies for when you need them. Keep them in mind. Refer to this book often.

Every day of your life, your free will will be tested. Don't be scared. You know how to make good decisions. Believe in yourself. Have faith in yourself. Trust yourself more with each passing day. You will make the right choices. You have the power to adjust and make new choices. Everything is going to be just fine. You are the best and most fertile soil. I know you get it. Soon enough you will know it, too.

TAG, you're it!

God Bless.

Appendix A ~

Specific Drug Details

The following Internet Web links provide detailed information about marijuana, LSD, ecstasy, and cocaine, including detailed information about the short-term and long-term effects of these drugs on your body.

Marijuana: http://www.usdoj.gov/dea/concern/marijuana.
    html
LSD: http://www.usdoj.gov/dea/concern/lsd.html
Ecstasy: http://www.usdoj.gov/dea/concern/mdma.html
Cocaine: http://www.usdoj.gov/dea/concern/cocaine.html

Appendix B ~

Sexual Assault—Steps to Take

Steps you should take right away if you or someone you know has been sexually assaulted:[24]

- Get away from the attacker to a safe place as fast as you can. Then call 911 or the police.
- Call a friend or family member you trust. You can also call a crisis center or a hotline to talk with a counselor. One hotline is the National Sexual Assault Hotline at 800-656-HOPE (4673). Feelings of shame, guilt, fear, and shock are normal. It is important to get counseling from a trusted professional.
- Do not wash, comb, or clean any part of your body. Do not change clothes, if possible, so the hospital staff can collect evidence. Do not touch or change anything at the scene of the assault.
- Go to your nearest hospital emergency room as soon as possible. You need to be examined, treated for any injuries, and screened for possible sexually transmitted diseases (STDs) or pregnancy. The doctor will collect evidence

using a rape kit for fibers, hairs, saliva, semen, or clothing that the attacker may have left behind. You should also ask about emergency contraception.

- You or the hospital staff can call the police from the emergency room to file a report.
- Ask the hospital staff about possible support groups you can attend right away.
- Ask where else you can go for help.

There are many organizations and hotlines in every state and territory. These crisis centers and agencies work hard to stop assaults and help victims. You can find contact information for these organizations at:

- National Domestic Violence Hotline 1-800-799-SAFE (7233) or 1-800-787-3224 (TDD—Telecommunications device for the deaf)
- National Sexual Assault Hotline 1-800-656-HOPE (4673)
- http://www.womenshealth.gov/violence/state/

You also can obtain the numbers of shelters, counseling services, and legal assistance in your phone book.

Appendix C ~

Signs to Watch For

The following are short lists of signs to watch for.[25] The lists are not exhaustive and are not a substitute for medical advice.

For eating disorders, signs can include:
- Secrecy surrounding eating and the time period after eating
- Frequent trips to the bathroom for purging after meals of bingeing
- Signs and smells of vomiting
- Avoidance of eating with others
- Eating large amounts of food with no apparent change in weight
- Weight loss.

For alcoholism, signs can include:
- Drinking alone or in secret
- Drinking to feel "normal"
- Finding excuses to drink

- Inability to reduce or stop alcohol intake
- Not remembering conversations or commitments
- Becoming angry when being confronted about drinking.

For an abusive relationship, signs can include someone who:
- Acts excessively jealous or possessive toward you
- Tries to control you by being very bossy or demanding
- Tries to isolate you by demanding you cut off social contacts and friendships
- Is violent and/or loses his or her temper quickly
- Pressures you sexually or demands sexual activities you are not comfortable with
- Blames you when he or she mistreats you
- Has a history of bad relationships
- You've been warned about by your family and friends who are concerned for your safety or emotional well-being
- You frequently worry about in regard to how he or she will react to things you say or do
- Makes jokes that shame, humiliate, demean, or embarrass you, whether privately or around family and friends
- You have trouble ending the relationship with, even though you know inside it's the right thing to do.

For suicide, signs can include:
- Talking about dying—any mention of dying, disappearing, jumping, shooting oneself, or other types of self-harm.
- Change in personality—sad, withdrawn, irritable, anxious, tired, indecisive, apathetic.
- Change in behavior—can't concentrate on school, work, routine tasks.
- Fear of losing control—going crazy, harming self or others.

- Low self-esteem—feeling worthless, shame, overwhelming guilt, self-hatred, "everyone would be better off without me."
- No hope for the future—believing things will never get better, that nothing will ever change.
- Giving away favorite things.

Appendix D ~

A Friend in Need

No one is placed on the right path and expected to stay put. It takes something like turmoil at home, the stress to succeed academically, boyfriend or girlfriend problems, or trying to fit in at school for a person to question himself or herself, or to injure oneself, or inflict pain on others.

Girls tend to be critical of both themselves and others. At some point in your life, you will fall victim to gossip, stories, and teasing. It takes a strong person to stand up to a bully or admit his or her own mistakes, but it takes an even stronger person to stand up for a fellow classmate.

Whether it is a childhood friend, a fellow classmate, your sister, or even yourself, it is mandatory for you to recognize the signs of either self-inflicted abuse or abuse from another source. The most common self-inflicted injuries for girls will come in the form of cutting, eating disorders, or becoming victim to an abusive relationship. It is up to you, as a friend, to help those in need.

For cutters, you will become aware of their disorder when they start to wear long, dark clothing in order to hide both their wounds and blood. If a friend never wears jewelry, you should become suspicious when she suddenly wears armbands that she refuses to take off. The irritability and sudden secrecy of your fellow classmate reiterate the point that something is suddenly wrong.

If you believe someone you know is cutting herself, make sure to let the principal and school counselor know. Your friend's life and health are in jeopardy.

Every girl has at least one flaw that she is not proud of. As girls grow older, they experience an unexpected transformation in their bodies. The sudden change in hip size, bust size, and height can cause a girl to become overly self-conscious. Typically, girls in high school go on diets to watch their weight, but when a diet goes too far, it becomes your responsibly to alert an elder of your friend's dwindling pant size.

I knew a girl, Gabriela, who was a straight-A student, beautiful, and popular with both girls and guys; however, she became self-conscious of her body her freshman year of high school. Although she weighed a healthy 130 pounds, she went away for the summer and came back her sophomore year weighing only 95 pounds!

She spent her sophomore year of high school in and out of rehab clinics. She was forced to go to the bathroom with a nurse to prove that she was not going to throw up her food. She spent days on an IV because she refused to eat. She had three minor heart attacks that year because her heart was slowly being broken down by lack of nutrients. Because of her heart condition, she was unable to play sports at school, and she got behind in her schoolwork because of her constant stays in rehab.

Gabriela will never fully recover from her disorder, and though she has not gone back to rehab since her sophomore year, her heart and body are no longer the same. Gabriela is at high risk for further heart attacks at a young age, arthritis, weak bones, loss of hair, premature wrinkles, and stunted growth. It's one thing to diet; it's another to nearly die from it.

If your friend disappears during lunch, has too much homework, never attends meals, is irritable, and is suddenly shrinking in size, you NEED to alert a grown-up. Her life depends on you standing up to protect her.

No matter how much your classmate may hate you for telling on her, she will respect your decision in the long run for saving her life.

Relationships can be difficult for any person. Whether you're young or old, dating will always be complicated. However, if a classmate admits he or she is gay, especially in high school, he or she encounters even greater difficultly in relationships.

If someone is honest enough to admit being gay, it becomes your responsibility to respect that person's honesty and choice. Your classmate isn't any different now than before the admission. As a friend, you need to respect people no matter what their race, religion, or sexual orientation may be.

A girl told me a story about a lesbian couple at her school. Everyone at the school, even the administration, respected the same-sex relationship.

The couple spent two years dating; however, it wasn't until senior year that the friends of the couple began to question Wendy, the "dom" (more masculine lesbian), and her interaction with her partner Julie. Everyone at school knew that

Wendy had a temper, but no one was aware that Julie had become Wendy's punching bag.

Three months before the senior graduation, Wendy and Julie had a very public argument. When the argument escalated, the couple was told to go to a different room and resolve the issue. Julie came back with a black eye and bloody arm.

Julie's friends sat down with the administration and told the school of the abuse that Julie had endured for the past two years. Wendy was suspended and unable to participate in graduation. Julie was finally safe.

An abusive relationship can happen to anyone. Whether it is physical or mental abuse, it is up to you to make it stop. Whoever is enduring the abuse is probably too afraid to leave the relationship; it becomes your responsibility to protect your classmate in need. Tell a parent, friend, teacher, or school counselor. Make your friend safe. You could be saving her life.

It is up to girls to protect one another. Whether it is a friend, classmate, or someone you have never met, make sure to help in every way you can.

Appendix E ~

Take Some Time
by Andrew Dudum

You tell me what's right, I must be wrong. I just don't see.

You figured it out, where I belong. That's just not me.

I've got to take some time to remind myself. Close my eyes and breathe.

Figure out who I am inside, and where I want to be.

It's not that I want to disagree or raise my voice.

I'm trying real hard for you to see that it's my choice.

I've got to take some time to remind myself. Close my eyes and breathe.

Figure out who I am inside. And where I want to be.

I've got to take some time to remind myself. Close my eyes and breathe.

Figure out who I am inside. And where I want to be.

Endnotes ~

¹ kdhnews.com. Flaccus, Gillian, "L.A. Catholic Diocese Could Settle Hundreds of Abuse Claims," [http://www.kdhnews.com/news/story.aspx?id=16665] (accessed 6/18/2007).

² New York Times, METRO NEWS BRIEFS: NEW JERSEY; Girls' Coach Admits Molesting 7 Players [http://query.nytimes.com/gst/fullpage.html?res=9F0CE7DC143BF930A15752C0A96E958260] (accessed 7/23/1998).

³ S.F.GATE.com. Williams, Lance, "Police Official to Order Probe in Zapping Case" [http://sfgate.com/cgi-bin/article.cgi?f=/c/a/2007/05/26/BAGLRQ2AGA1.DTL&hw=police+excessive+force&sn+003&sc=683] (accessed 5/26/2007).

⁴ S.F.GATE.com. Coté, John, "Teacher Sentenced in Underage Sex Case" [http://www.sfgate.com/cgi-bin/article.cgi?f=/c/a/2007/08/03/BAKRRC7GT3.DTL&hw=san+bruno&sn=001&sc=1000] (accessed 8/3/2007).

⁵ [http://en.wikipedia.org/wiki/Jennifer_Moore] [http://missingexploited.com/2006/07/28/jennifer-moore-18-new-jersey-girl-abducted-beaten-and-killed/] (accessed 8/27/2007).

⁶ DAILY NEWS Burke, Kerry; Gendar, Alison; Moore, Robert, "Girl: Attacked after SoHo partying", [http://www.rhythmism.com/forum/showthread.php?t=42287] (accessed 8/10/2006).

⁷ [http://en.wikipedia.org/wiki/Natalee_Holloway] (accessed 8/25/2007).

[8] Sobering Statistics, [http://hcs.calpoly.edu/peerhealth/alcohol/info_students_stats.html]

[9] "Facts on Sex Education in the United States," Guttmacher Institute, [http://www.guttmacher.org/pubs/fb_sexEd2006.html] 12/2006

[10] Weinstock, H et al., Sexually transmitted diseases among American youth: incidence and prevalence estimates, 2000, Perspectives on Sexual and Reproductive Health, 2004, 36(1):6–10.; Darroch, JE, Frost, JJ and Singh, S, Teenage Sexual and Reproductive Behavior in Developed Countries: Can More Progress Be Made?, Occasional Report, New York: The Alan Guttmacher Institute, 2001, No. 3. Source: Alan Guttmacher Institute, "Teen Sex and Pregnancy," fact sheet, agi-usa.org/pubs/19/1999; "Teen Sex Overview" [http://www.teencarecenter.org/index.php?s=factsheets&p=sheet8]

[11] Source: Alan Guttmacher Institute, Teenage pregnancy: overall trends and state-by-state information, New York: AGI, 1999, Table 1; and Henshaw SK, U.S. Teenage pregnancy statistics with comparative statistics for women aged 20- 24, New York: AGI, 1999, p. 5. "Teen Sex Overview" [http://www.teencarecenter.org/index.php?s=factsheets&p=sheet8]

[12] Rape, Abuse and Incest National Network, National Crime Victimization Survey, 2005 [http://www.rainn.org/statistics/index.html?gclid=CLqugYLtlY4CFSDyYAodJETLjg] (accessed 2006).

[13] The Hathor Legacy 2005-2007. Greenberg, Jerrold S., Clint E. Bruess, and Debra W. Haffner. Exploring the Dimensions of Human Sexuality. (Greenberg, Bruess and Haffner, 572) Sudbury, MA. Jones and Bartlett Publishers, 2000. Lips, Hilary M. Sex & Gender: An Introduction. Fourth Ed. Mountain View, CA. Mayfield Publishing Company, 2001. (Lips, 233) [http://thehathorlegacy.info/rape-statistics/]

[14] I Speak of Dreams., Duni, Michael, Michael Duni: "Another High School Student Dies of Alcohol Overdose," [http://lizditz.typepad.com/i_speak_of_dreams/2004/12/michael_duni_16.html] (accessed12/14/2004).

[15] Ventura County Star. Foxman, Adam; Koehler, Tamara, Ventura County Star, "Drug Mix May Have Killed Teen in Ventura," [http://www.

venturacountystar.com/news (accessed 4/13/2007). /2007/apr/13/drug-mix-may-have-killed-teen-in-ventura/] (accessed 4/13/2007).

[16] Southern Methodist University. [http://en.wikipedia.org/wiki/Southern_Methodist_University] (accessed 6/29/2007).

[17] 4woman.gov. "U.S. Department of Health & Human Services womenshealth.gov," [http://www.4woman.gov/faq/sexualassault.htm] (accessed January 2005).

[18] S.F.Gate.com. Egelko, Bob, "MySpace Hookup Leads to Arrest" http://www.sfgate.com/cgi-bin/article.cgi?f=/c/a/2007/08/12/BAVTRH7RA.DTL&hw=myspace+hookup&sn=001&sc=1000 (accessed 8/12/2007).

[19] freerepublic.com. Ogles, Malena, "Free Republic Mother, & Unborn Child Killed, 6 yr. Old Girl Injured," [http://www.freerepublic.com/focus/f-chat/1856619/posts] (accessed 6/27/2007).

[20] Msnbc.com. Shenfeld, Hilar, "My Mother, My Bartender," [http://www.msnbc.msn.com/id/19251324/site/newsweek/] (accessed 6/15/2007).

[21] S.F.Gate.com. Nevius, C.W., "Alleged Rape Victim's Rescuers Threatened," [http://www.sfgate.com/cgi-bin/article.cgi?f=/c/a/2007/06/03/MNG7EQ6QJ81.DTL&feed=rss.news] (accessed 6/3/2007).

[22] Gibran, Khalil [http://www.quotedb.com/authors/kahlil-gibran]

[23] Gibran, Khalil "The Prophet" (on Marriage)

[24] 4woman.gov. "U.S. Department of Health & Human Services womenshealth.gov," [http://www.4woman.gov/faq/sexualassault.htm] (accessed January 2005).

[25] 4woman.gov. "U.S. Department of Health & Human Services womenshealth.gov," [http://www.4woman.gov/faq/sexualassault.htm] (accessed January 2005).